# The Merchant of Venice

## William Shakespeare

## Guide written by
## John Mahoney

A *Letts* Literature Guide

First published 1994
Reprinted 1994

Letts Educational
Aldine House
Aldine Place
London W12 8AW

**Text** © John Mahoney and Stewart Martin 1994

**Typeset by** Jordan Publishing Design

**Self-test questions devised by** Claire Wright

**Text design** Jonathan Barnard

**Cover and text illustrations** Hugh Marshall

**Graphic illustration** Ian Foulis and Associates, Barbara Linton

Design © BPP (Letts Educational) Ltd

ISBN 1 85758 251 9

**British Library Cataloguing in Publication Data**
A CIP record for this book is available from the British Library.

Printed and bound in Great Britain by
Ashford Colour Press Ltd, Gosport, Hants

Letts Educational is the trading name of BPP (Letts Educational) Ltd

# ■ Contents

# Plot synopsis

Bassanio, a Venetian gentleman, has spent all his money. He wishes to mend his fortunes by marrying Portia, a rich heiress who lives in Belmont. His friend Antonio, The Merchant of Venice, is willing to help him but all his money is tied up in ships trading across the world. Antonio agrees to use his own good name to secure his friend a loan of three thousand ducats.

Shylock, a Jewish moneylender, agrees to lend Antonio the money. However, because he hates Antonio, he imposes the condition that if the money is not repaid in three months' time Antonio must forfeit a pound of his flesh, to be cut from wherever Shylock wishes.

In the meantime, Shylock's daughter Jessica elopes with Lorenzo, a Christian gentleman. Bassanio goes to Belmont and wins Portia for his bride. His friend Gratiano marries Portia's maid, Nerissa. However, news comes that Antonio's ventures have failed and he is brought to trial by Shylock, who claims his pound of flesh. Portia and her maid, Nerissa, exchange rings with their husbands, who vow never to part with them.

Bassanio hurries back to Venice to be with his friend. Portia and her maid, disguised as lawyer and clerk, arrive to defend Antonio. In court, Shylock is defeated because the bond does not allow for any blood to be taken, only flesh. Because his action threatened the life of a Venetian, he loses his goods. He is also forced to become a Christian. Portia and Nerissa, still disguised, persuade Bassanio and Gratiano to give them the rings in payment for saving Antonio.

Triumphant, everyone returns to Belmont, where it is learned that Antonio's ships are safe. After some light-hearted argument, the rings are returned to their rightful owners and the play ends on a happy note.

# ◼ Characters and themes

## Antonio

is The Merchant of Venice. A lonely figure, he is prepared to give all to help his friend Bassanio. At the start of the play he offers his flesh in a bond for his friend; at the end, he offers his soul.

## Bassanio

seems to be an unreliable spendthrift, but he matures, shows a deal of good judgement and marries Portia.

## Portia

A wealthy lady of Belmont, Portia has too much time and wealth on her hands at the beginning. She shows herself to be honest (to her father's wishes), witty and intelligent. She defends Antonio expertly, but whilst proclaiming the need for mercy, does not show much to Shylock.

## Shylock

is a stock Jewish figure set up to be knocked down. He hates Antonio, who undermines his business by lending money free of interest. Driven by hatred and a desire to get rid of Antonio, he designs the pound of flesh bond. However, the law which he invokes finally frustrates his desires, and he ends up penniless and alone.

## Major plots

These are the pound of flesh bond between Antonio and Shylock and the casket test for Portia's hand in marriage which Bassanio succeeds in.

## Minor plots

These are the elopement of Jessica, Shylock's daughter, with Lorenzo and the ring plot between Portia, Nerissa and their husbands.

## Major themes

These centre around love and friendship versus greed, and mercy versus justice. The love and friendship shown by characters such as Antonio, Bassanio, Portia and Jessica is contrasted with the overwhelming greed of Shylock. Centred on his bond with Antonio, greed pervades all his relationships and dealings with the other characters. Finally, it brings about his downfall. The central theme of the trial is the contrast between justice or law, and mercy. Shylock demands justice and spurns mercy, and justice is all he finally gets. Portia pleads for justice to be tempered with mercy, but in the end she gives Shylock justice without mercy.

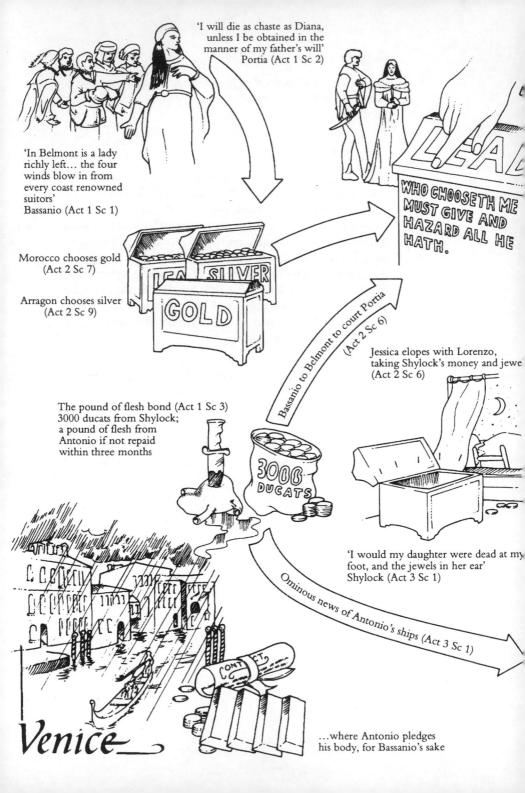

'I will die as chaste as Diana, unless I be obtained in the manner of my father's will' Portia (Act 1 Sc 2)

'In Belmont is a lady richly left... the four winds blow in from every coast renowned suitors' Bassanio (Act 1 Sc 1)

WHO CHOOSETH ME MUST GIVE AND HAZARD ALL HE HATH.

Morocco chooses gold (Act 2 Sc 7)

Arragon chooses silver (Act 2 Sc 9)

Bassanio to Belmont to court Portia (Act 2 Sc 6)

Jessica elopes with Lorenzo, taking Shylock's money and jewe[ls] (Act 2 Sc 6)

The pound of flesh bond (Act 1 Sc 3) 3000 ducats from Shylock; a pound of flesh from Antonio if not repaid within three months

3000 DUCATS

'I would my daughter were dead at my foot, and the jewels in her ear' Shylock (Act 3 Sc 1)

Ominous news of Antonio's ships (Act 3 Sc 1)

*Venice*

...where Antonio pledges his body, for Bassanio's sake

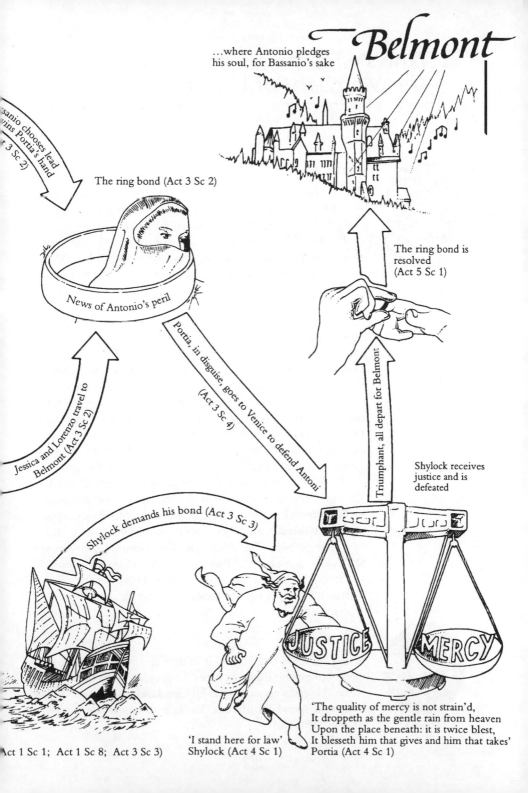

*Belmont*

…where Antonio pledges his soul, for Bassanio's sake

…sanio chooses lead …wins Portia's hand (…t 3 Sc 2)

The ring bond (Act 3 Sc 2)

News of Antonio's peril

The ring bond is resolved (Act 5 Sc 1)

Jessica and Lorenzo travel to Belmont (Act 3 Sc 2)

Portia, in disguise, goes to Venice to defend Antoni (Act 3 Sc 4)

Triumphant, all depart for Belmont

Shylock receives justice and is defeated

Shylock demands his bond (Act 3 Sc 3)

JUSTICE   MERCY

…Act 1 Sc 1;   Act 1 Sc 8;   Act 3 Sc 3)

'I stand here for law' Shylock (Act 4 Sc 1)

'The quality of mercy is not strain'd,
It droppeth as the gentle rain from heaven
Upon the place beneath: it is twice blest,
It blesseth him that gives and him that takes'
Portia (Act 4 Sc 1)

# Who's who in
# *The Merchant of Venice*

Antonio

## Antonio

Antonio is the Merchant of Venice of the play's title. His speech which begins 'In sooth I know not why I am so sad, it wearies me' sets the scene for the events that will befall him during most of the play. Why is he sad? It is a device used by Shakespeare to set the initial mood of the play. Perhaps his sadness also reflects the mood of other rich Venetian merchants who had everything: note how the rich heiress, Portia, also declares that she is weary. Most likely Antonio is sad because he knows that the close relationship he has with Bassanio is about to be upset by the latter's wish to seek Portia's hand in marriage.

Despite the fact that the play is named after him, Antonio plays a very small, though important part in it. He exemplifies the limits to which love and friendship may be taken. In agreeing to finance Bassanio's pursuit of Portia he provides for the disruption of his own deep relationship with Bassanio. Having no finances available, he is quite prepared to use his good name to seek money for his friend, and then to agree a forfeit that puts his life in jeopardy as security for the loan.

Antonio stands in contrast to Shylock's calculating greed. He is melancholy, passive in his acceptance of events affecting his life, somewhat unemotional in response to the threat to his life and is ultimately a lonely figure when surrounded at the end by happy couples. The other side of his nature is seen from Shylock's descriptions of how he spat upon Shylock's beard and under-mined his business practices. However, he does perhaps reflect the ideal of selfless generosity which is the play's central theme.

Bassanio

## Bassanio

When we meet Bassanio he is in debt and wants to borrow money to pursue Portia in order 'to get clear of all the debts I owe'. He gives no security to his friend and when he gets the money, he spends it on liveries for his servants and a party: not an auspicious start.

He must have good points. Antonio is certainly prepared to trust him: witness the bond he enters. Bassanio does show some sensitivity to the matter of asking for yet more money: his archery image (Act 1, Sc 1) suggests he feels he ought to justify his request. And he warns Antonio against the bond, so he shows some sense, though he still accepts the money!

When departing for Belmont he agrees to take his friend Gratiano along, despite believing him to be rude and wild – not quite the person to go with on such a delicate mission. This is either a very generous, or foolhardy gesture on his part.

Nerissa calls him a 'scholar and a soldier'. His choice of the correct casket, lead, indicates that he is more of a thinker, not easily taken in by appearances. There seems no doubt that he genuinely loves Portia and he is honest about his debt to Antonio. On hearing of the latter's trouble he goes immediately to assist him and shows his concern throughout the trial. He is seen to be a very different man at the end of the play to the man we met at the beginning.

## Shylock

Shylock

Shylock demonstrates the stock features of the Elizabethan caricature of a Jew: hatred of Christians and the practice of usury (lending money out at interest). This latter is something which our society virtually lives by but the Elizabethans had rather different views. Although his name has become equated with the warped greed of the miser, few who read the play can help feeling some degree of sympathy with his misfortunes.

He demonstrates a quite unyielding hatred of Antonio and all he stands for. The bottom line for Shylock appears to be profit and in order to pursue that profit he is prepared to take a short-term monetary loss, 3000 ducats, so that he can kill Antonio and practice usury without competition. This side of Shylock does not make the audience like him!

Shylock's description of how Antonio has abused and spat on him, and deliberately undermined his business serves to redress the balance a little in his favour. His daughter's elopement with a Christian and the theft of his money and jewels also give us pause for thought about our attitude towards him. However, the comic way in which he is presented as reacting to this event and his cry of 'my ducats', evoke laughter, not sympathy.

His famous speech 'If you prick us' (Act 2, Sc 1) again makes us reconsider our attitudes towards him, but then he spoils his plea by using it to justify plain revenge. The trial scene shows him at his worst. He came prepared with his own scales to weigh the flesh and a knife which he keeps sharpening, determined to cut the flesh himself. He rejects any plea for justice to be tempered by mercy. His observation when asked about a surgeon – that the bond did not require it – is cruel. When justice is eventually served and Shylock gets the sharp end, he has lost the audience's sympathy. Even Portia's failure to be merciful to him does not upset us unduly.

Portia

## Portia

Like Antonio, Portia is weary, but her weariness is perhaps derived from her lack of control over the choice of her future husband. She remains loyal to her father's will, and accepts that her husband will be the one who chooses the correct casket. Like Antonio she is passive at the start of the play, but she emerges as a sensitive lover of Bassanio and a mature defender of Antonio.

She demonstrates some wit and accurate observation when she describes her various suitors. She is openly hostile to the Prince of Morocco's dark features, but willing to marry him if he chooses the correct casket.

When Bassanio reveals his friend's misfortune, Portia is quick to offer her support and does not try to stop Bassanio returning to Venice. Indeed, secretly, she joins him disguised as a lawyer. There she proceeds to defend Antonio. She shows herself to be resourceful and commanding. She clearly and cleverly expounds the law, leading Shylock gently along the path towards his own destruction. By gaining Shylock's utter determination to have just the letter of the law, justice without mercy, she opens the way for the same to be applied to him. However, she disregards her own eloquent plea about the quality of mercy when she sentences Shylock.

When back in Belmont, she again demands the letter of the law of Bassanio in the ring plot, but then immediately shows him the mercy that was not available to Shylock in Venice.

Portia's love for Bassanio and, therefore, for his friend Antonio, overpowers Shylock's greed and defeats his deadly intent. Like Antonio and Bassanio, she demonstrates the power of love and friendship over greed.

## Gratiano

Companion to Bassanio and Antonio, Gratiano 'speaks an infinite deal of nothing'; he is 'too wild, too rude, and bold of voice'. He is taken with Bassanio to Belmont which shows the power of Bassanio's friendship – he could well have judged it better not to take Gratiano on such a delicate mission. His marriage to Nerissa both echoes and emphasises the love of Portia and Bassanio.

To a certain extent he acts as a contrast to Bassanio: note his more casual attitude to the ring plot and how at the trial scene he shows an ugly side when baiting the desperate Shylock. Bassanio's behaviour is more dignified and concerned.

## Jessica

Shylock's daughter Jessica plays only a small part in the play. She demonstrates the power of love by being prepared to abandon not only her father but also her religion. However, she also offends against two of the Ten Commandments when she dishonours her father by wishing she were not his daughter and by stealing his money and jewels.

Her casual use of Shylock's money, as reported by Tubal, infuriates Shylock and leads to the description of Shylock bemoaning his loss publicly, much to the amusement of all. It lessens the impact of what she has done and helps to bias the audience against her father.

The lyrical poetry of her scenes with Lorenzo epitomises the supremacy of love and as such underpins a vital theme of the play.

## Lorenzo

A friend of Antonio and Bassanio, Lorenzo, by eloping with and marrying Jessica, helps towards Shylock's downfall.

## Nerissa

The maid and companion of Portia, Nerissa has a small part to play. Her marriage to Gratiano and participation in the ring plot echo the more important relationship between Portia and Bassanio.

## Launcelot

Initially servant to Shylock, Launcelot soon enters the service of Bassanio, thus adding to the gradual isolation of Shylock.

The scenes with his father provide some comic relief, as does his soliloquy when he debates whether to leave Shylock's service. These scenes also have the effect of undermining Shylock and so expose him to the audience's dislike.

## Old Gobbo

Launcelot's father, Old Gobbo, has little real part to play, except to give Launcelot the opportunity to 'sound off' about Shylock.

## Tubal

A fellow Jew, Tubal provides the money for the bond. Despite being of the same race, he does not seem to have much sympathy for Shylock. Rather, he seems to enjoy Shylock's unhappiness and discomfort when he regales him with details of how Jessica spends Shylock's money: he carefully uses this bad news to balance the news of Antonio's misfortunes.

## Salerio and Solanio

Two gentlemen of Venice whose main function is to serve as commentators on events and bearers of news.

## The Prince of Morocco and the Prince of Arragon

Suitors to Portia, they both fail to choose the correct casket and in doing so demonstrate their concern with appearance rather than reality, and their arrogance and high opinion of themselves. They serve as stark contrasts to the sensitive and thoughtful approach of Bassanio to the same task, and highlight his worthiness to be Portia's husband.

## Various suitors of Portia

We have to rely on Portia for our knowledge of them. They only serve to demonstrate her wit and observation of character.

## The Duke of Venice

The trial 'judge', he has little part to play except to ensure that the law is upheld. What is interesting is that he does not expect Shylock to demonstrate mercy, but he asks for it nevertheless. However, at the end of the trial he is quick to show mercy to Shylock, offering him his life without any hesitation – in contrast to Gratiano and Portia.

# ■ Themes, bonds, plots and subplots

**Love versus greed**

## Love and friendship versus greed

The play is a demonstration of the triumph of how love and friendship overcome greed. Shylock epitomises greed. His conversations with first Bassanio and then Antonio show that he hates Christians because they frustrate his greed. His first words in the play are: 'Three thousand ducats…'. He says he hates Antonio because 'he lends out money gratis, and brings down the rate of usance here in Venice', depriving Shylock of greater profit.

Shylock willingly parts with the services of Launcelot as he is 'snail-slow in profit'. To Tubal (Act 3, end of Sc 1) he openly admits: 'I will have the heart of him (Antonio) if he forfeit, for were he out of Venice I can make what merchandise I will.' Without Antonio to undercut his rate of interest, Shylock will be free to charge whatever he likes.

When his daughter elopes and takes his money and jewels, it is this theft, rather than his daughter's fate, that concerns him. The trial scene epitomises the depths of his greed. Deaf to all pleas for mercy, he has his knife and scales ready to cut and weigh Antonio's flesh.

In contrast to Shylock's greed, there is the love and friendship demonstrated by the three other main characters. Antonio loves his friend Bassanio so much that he is prepared to put his life at the mercy of his enemy, Shylock. He even seems willing to believe that Shylock might change: 'I lie thee gentle Jew/The Hebrew will turn Christian: he grows kind' – a misjudgement, but kindly thought. His loan to Bassanio hurts his own heart, because it takes Bassanio away from him. When writing to Bassanio to explain his predicament, he requests only that he might have a last chance to see his friend before dying.

Bassanio knows that he can call upon Antonio's friendship to help him pursue Portia, even though he is already in debt to him. His friendship for Gratiano overcomes his better judgement, and he agrees that he may go to Belmont with him.

He is honest in his love for Portia, which quickly overtakes his earlier sentiment: 'to pay off all the debts I owe'. His love for Antonio brings him back to Venice where he offers his own life: 'The Jew shall have my flesh, blood, bones and all/Ere thou shalt lose for me one drop of blood.' Bassanio's love for Portia makes him extremely reluctant to part with her ring, and he does so only when pressed by Antonio.

Portia's love for Bassanio includes his friends. She offers her wealth to help Antonio, then departs in disguise for Venice in order to save his life. Her love for Bassanio leads her to Venice where she overcomes Shylock. Finally, she forgives Bassanio for parting with her ring, re-emphasising that love and forgiveness are superior to self-centred greed.

## Mercy versus justice and the law

Mercy versus justice

The trial scene is central to this aspect of the play. We are forewarned of Shylock's view: 'tell me not of mercy' (Act 3 Sc 3). He wants only justice: 'The Duke shall grant me justice.' And Antonio recognises he will get nothing from Shylock: 'I'll follow him no more with bootless (unproductive) prayers.'

As the trial scene opens (Act 4), the Duke judges Shylock 'an inhuman wretch, uncapable of pity, void, and empty from any dram of mercy.' Nevertheless, the Duke asks him to show mercy – but Shylock demands his bond. When he has rejected many more ducats than called for by the bond, the Duke wonders: 'How shalt thou hope for mercy, rend'ring none?' It is here that the court's merciless persecution of Shylock, once he has lost his case, finds some of its justification.

When Portia arrives, she quickly assesses the facts and declares that, if Antonio is not to die, 'Then must the Jew be merciful.' Her speech extols the virtue of mercy: 'The quality of mercy is not strain'd...' (Act 4 Sc 1), but Shylock is interested only in revenge and Antonio's death.

Portia cleverly leads Shylock to reiterate his demand for law and justice. More money is offered and rejected. When Portia suggests a surgeon should be there to stop the blood so that Antonio does not bleed to death, Shylock objects that this was not part of the bond. But the simple, blind administration of the law which is what Shylock wants will not give him his revenge or Antonio's life: instead, without mercy, it takes from him his wealth and his religion.

Portia is as merciless as Shylock in her administration of the law. Antonio shows mercy, as does the Duke. It is perhaps significant that when Portia returns to Belmont she shows forgiveness and mercy.

## The pound of flesh bond

**The pound of flesh bond**

Antonio enters into a bond with Shylock. In return for 3000 ducats which he wants for his friend Bassanio, he agrees to repay the money within three months or allow Shylock to cut a pound of flesh from anywhere on his body. His ventures seem to fail and Shylock claim his forfeit. In court, Shylock's desire for the law rebounds on him, and he loses all.

## The casket test

**The casket test**

Portia's father has decreed in his will that she must marry the man who selects the correct one of three caskets made of gold, silver and lead. He judged that Portia would love a man who can distinguish between apparent worth and real worth. Bassanio chooses the correct casket, lead, and marries Portia.

## The elopement

**The elopement**

Jessica, Shylock's daughter, has fallen in love with a Christian gentleman, Lorenzo. She decides to elope, taking Shylock's money and jewels. She, with Launcelot who also leaves Shylock's house, begins the gradual process of stripping Shylock of everything he possesses.

## The ring bond

**The ring bond**

When Portia and Nerissa marry, they give rings to their husbands, who swear never to part with them. After the trial, both men are persuaded to give the rings to the lawyer and his clerk. Returning to Belmont, Portia and Nerissa ask where their rings are. They accuse their husbands of being unfaithful to their vows, but finally admit that *they* were the lawyer and clerk in disguise, and forgive their husbands.

## The last bond

Antonio offers his soul to Portia in forfeit should Bassanio ever betray her trust in him.

# ■ Text commentary

## Act 1 Scene 1

*We meet Antonio, the merchant of Venice of the title. He appears to be unhappy, for reasons that are not clear. His friend Bassanio, wants to borrow money from him so that he can pursue Portia, a rich heiress. Antonio agrees, but will himself have to borrow the money, as all his wealth is tied up in trade.*

### Antonio's sadness 'wearies' him

Antonio

'What stuff 'tis made of, whereof it is born, I am to learn;' No reason is given here or later for Antonio's sadness. Perhaps he has a premonition of problems to come, but almost certainly his love for and close friendship with Bassanio will be affected by the latter's pursuit of Portia. (Do not allow twentieth-century interpretations of a loving friendship between men as being almost necessarily homosexual over-influence your judgement of their relationship.) The play has much to do with the concept of love, in its purest sense, versus greed, with Antonio and Shylock personifying the theme.

The 'want-wit' that Antonio accuses himself of in this scene will in a way be fulfilled when he enters into the bond with Shylock.

### Prophecies of disaster for Antonio's ships

The words of Solanio and Salerio where they stress the dangers and worries of being in Antonio's position are very prophetic. Antonio's trading ventures will appear to fail and Shylock will pursue him in court for satisfaction of the bond between them.

However, Antonio gives three reasons why his ventures do not worry him: his goods are not all in one ship, nor are they concentrated in one place, and the results of this year's trading will not decide the fate of his fortunes. Nevertheless, the idea that his ships may be endangered is firmly planted in this scene. Also note that in the strength of his rebuttal about his prospects for fortune, he does not make his two friends aware of how short of money he is – a fact that he will disclose only to Bassanio.

### Antonio denies he is in love

Antonio rejects the suggestion that he is in love, and so we still have no good explanation of his sadness. This sadness acts as a foil for the lightheartedness of his companions. In a similar way, Antonio's trial will act as a background and contrast to the various romances.

### 'A stage where every man must play a part'

Antonio

Antonio's words to Gratiano, 'A stage where every man must play a part,/And mine a sad one.' restate his feelings and reflect events to come. At almost every turn misfortune dogs him, and even at the end, when Shylock loses his case and his ships return home, Antonio seems to stand apart from the love and happiness that his companions enjoy.

Gratiano's comment, 'Let me play the fool' finds its reflection in others' opinions of him. Bassanio seems to have a low opinion of him but still allows friendship to overcome his judgement when put to the test later in the play. Bassanio's assessment of Gratiano is that he 'speaks an infinite deal of nothing'. He is also tactless – he has to be dragged away by Lorenzo to allow Bassanio and Antonio to talk privately. Bassanio gives further comments on his character later, in Act 2 Sc 2.

### Antonio asks about Portia

When Gratiano departs, Antonio immediately taxes Bassanio with a question about the 'secret pilgrimage' to a lady. Perhaps here lies the secret of his sadness. His friendship with Bassanio is obviously very close, and maybe it is the thought of losing that closeness which makes him sad.

### Bassanio, in debt to Antonio and in love with Portia

Bassanio

Love versus greed

Bassanio ignores Antonio's question and launches straight into an account of his money problems. The 'secret pilgrimage' turns into a way 'to get clear of all the debts I owe'. Be aware, however, that whilst this is an immediate consideration for Bassanio, it is not his sole reason for pursuing Portia: he does love her. To Elizabethans, the idea of marrying for fortune was not unusual, nor was it a practice to be condemned. That Bassanio feels able to turn to his friend for a loan demonstrates the closeness of their relationship and the extent to which money becomes subservient to love.

Bassanio wants to borrow money to 'catch' a rich heiress. Money is a theme that features in the relationships of all the characters in the play. Venice, the setting, is a centre of wealth, trade, money-lending and greed, and here the drama of love versus greed and mercy versus justice is played out.

Bassanio

Antonio

Bassanio is more than just a good-hearted spendthrift, as events will show. Here, his conversation with Antonio indicates that he is embarrassed at having to ask for yet more money and he therefore does not come straight to the point.

### Antonio pledges all to Bassanio

Antonio admits his cash problems to Bassanio but his love for his friend overcomes the natural caution of a merchant: he is willing to allow his good name to be used to obtain credit. It is in this scene that the events leading to the strange bond agreement, between Antonio and Shylock, have their origins.

Antonio is a wealthy merchant, but he is short of cash. However, he is obviously trusted and his name should be good enough on its own for a loan. His sadness in this opening scene is not clearly explained but it seems reasonable to assume that it is connected with Bassanio's pursuit of Portia. It is clear from his conversation that he was aware of the affair from the very beginning of the play. He reacts sharply to Bassanio trying to justify his request for yet another loan and thereby indicates the great depth of his love for him. In Antonio's eyes, Bassanio should never have been in any doubt that he would get his loan.

---

**Salerio and Solanio** are not important characters but they do serve a useful function of informing the audience about various matters and assisting the play to develop. Here they let the audience know that Antonio is a wealthy and successful merchant, and that all Antonio's wealth is at risk at sea.

**Venice and Belmont** are places of contrast. Here we see Venice as the seat of trade and money. It is where greed, usury and revenge will play their ugly parts. Love will find its fulfilment in Belmont. In Venice, Antonio's love for Bassanio will be frustrated but, perversely, it is Venice's money which will help Bassanio's love on its way.

**Remember** the sacrifice that Antonio is prepared to make for his friend, and note the extent to which Bassanio feels their friendship allows him to call yet again on Antonio's goodwill.

**Recall** the implied threat to Antonio's ships. Their disappearance will be crucial to the plot's development.

---

# Act 1 Scene 2

*Portia discusses her father's will: she must marry the man who chooses the correct one of three caskets. She and her maid, Nerissa, humorously discuss some recent suitors. Bassanio is mentioned as a possible suitor, and the arrival of the Prince of Morocco is announced.*

## Like Antonio, Portia is 'aweary', but she knows why

Here in Belmont, the concerns are not those of the merchants but of a father's desire for his daughter's happiness; rather different from Shylock's major interest – profit. But Portia is wearied by the thought that she might be forced to marry someone whom she does not love, and by the uncertainty that causes.

**Portia**

## The bond which binds Portia

Portia discusses her father's will with her maid and companion, Nerissa. It requires any suitor to choose between three caskets made from lead, silver and gold. Again the idea of wealth features, in that judgements are to be made about value and worth – but in this case the judgements also relate to love. However, the suitors have their own views as to whose worth is being judged, theirs or Portia's. This casket bond – for a bond is what the will amounts to – reflects the pound of flesh bond that will be entered into by Antonio. However, the

bond between father and daughter has only love and happiness as its motivating force, whilst the bond between Shylock and Antonio has hatred and revenge on Shylock's part, and love for his friend on Antonio's part. One is made in Belmont and the other in Venice. Contrast also Portia's father's love for his daughter with Shylock's love for Jessica.

**The casket test** Note how these two places are distinct: Belmont is a place of music and love; Venice a place of greed and threatened disaster.

## Portia shows her mettle

Portia and Nerissa discuss the various dignitaries who have visited Belmont and desired to marry Portia. Portia's assessment of the men's characters show her as perceptive and incisively witty, with a sharp eye for detail. When she takes up Antonio's case later in the play she demonstrates a great deal of mental agility and competence.

**Portia**

## Portia talks of Bassanio

The brief reference to Bassanio lets the audience know that Portia favours him: 'I remember him well, and I remember him worthy of thy praise.'

---

**The casket bond** introduced, but with little detail.

**Portia** is presented in a favourable light – witty and intelligent, but she is weary of the stream of unattractive suitors and the uncertainty imposed by her father's will

---

# Act 1 Scene 3

*An important scene in the play. We meet Shylock for the first time, discover his hatred for Antonio and Antonio's dislike of Shylock. The terms of the bond are agreed.*

### Bassanio negotiates a deal with Shylock – the bond

**The pound of flesh bond**

The bond, whereby Antonio will borrow three thousand ducats, which become repayable after three months, is negotiated by Bassanio. Shylock admits that Antonio is probably a 'good man' for the loan: his use of the word 'good' relates only to Antonio's ability to pay. However, he comments on the fact that Antonio's ships carry his wealth, and are easy prey to the perils of sea and man.

### Shylock shows his hatred

**Shylock**

Shylock declines to dine with Bassanio, and we quickly discover the depth of his hatred for Antonio. He hates him, 'for he is a Christian' – do not allow yourself to be convinced that the play is about religion and is anti-Semitic. Whilst Jews have often been used as stock figures for fun, and are equally associated with the acquisition of money and wealth, both aspects of which feature in this play, the central issues are of love against greed and mercy against justice.

Of much relevance in Shylock's speech, 'How like a fawning...' is Antonio's practice of lending money without interest. By adopting this practice, one that an Elizabethan audience would have accepted and approved, Antonio makes it difficult for money-lenders like Shylock to charge a high rate. An interesting aspect of the bond is that Shylock, like Antonio, will have to borrow the money himself to lend to Antonio. Tubal will loan the money to Shylock and one wonders perhaps what Shylock had to give Tubal as security.

### 'many a time and oft...'

**Antonio**

Note the parallels between Antonio and Shylock: both are seen as outsiders – Shylock is spurned by the Christians, and Antonio is often alone, in contrast to the loves being pursued by his companions. Shylock demonstrates his hatred for Antonio and, equally, Antonio shows himself to be virulent in his attitude towards and treatment of Shylock. The speech beginning, 'Signor Antonio, many a time and oft...' demonstrates the depth of feeling that underpins their antagonism for each other.

Antonio uses Shylock's hatred as bait to persuade him to make the loan – not that he needs much persuasion. After all, he suggests, if the money is not repaid

Shylock may exact a forfeit with an easy conscience if it is his enemy who has failed to fulfil the terms of the agreement. Bearing in mind Shylock's recent speech we must be suspicious of his motives when he suddenly declares, 'I would be friends with you and have your love'.

### The bond forfeit

The pound of
flesh bond

Love versus
greed

The penalty, or forfeit, to be exacted if Antonio fails to repay the three thousand ducats in three months' time is now explained by Shylock: a pound of flesh to be cut from any part of Antonio's body that Shylock wishes.

Antonio surely demonstrates a serious degree of 'want-wit' by agreeing to such a bond, though Bassanio recognises the dangers therein and protests that no agreement should be made. However, for Antonio's part, he is convinced that his ships will return in time and that he will be able to repay the bond. No doubt his love for Bassanio and a desire to help him also cloud his judgement in this matter. Shylock's comment that 'To buy his favour, I extend this friendship' is not only false in its declared intention but also fundamentally at odds with the reality of friendship/love – by its very nature it cannot be bought, only given.

### Premonitions of the future

Antonio's comments about Shylock becoming a Christian and growing kind completely misinterpret Shylock's motives and attitudes. Ironically, the 'Hebrew will turn Christian' (see the trial scene) – but not willingly.

### Appearance and reality

Shylock

A major theme that runs through the play relates to the fact that things are not always as they seem to be. In particular, we have just seen how Shylock has 'talked down' the significance of the pound of flesh forfeit, and how he says he wishes to buy Antonio's favour. The reality is that he sees the forfeit as a real threat to Antonio's life and has absolutely no desire for his friendship.

This theme is central to all the bonds in the play. Shylock really wants to profit from Antonio's death as he will be able to charge higher rates of interest when Antonio can no longer undercut him. The metal from which each casket is made disguises the reality of what it contains. The rings are not given away to strangers: in reality they stay with the married couples. Antonio offers his

**Bassanio**

final bond for Bassanio thinking his friend needs support when really there is no need.

Bassanio protests against the bond and shows his mistrust of Shylock but bows to Antonio's determination to help him. Antonio's judgement is perhaps blinded by an overwhelming desire to help Bassanio, regardless of cost or risk.

---

**The bond** is for three thousand ducats loaned for three months.

**The forfeit** is a pound of flesh to be cut from wherever Shylock desires on Antonio's body.

**Bassanio** shows himself more aware of Shylock's vengeful and dangerous nature than Antonio.

**Shylock and Antonio** demonstrate the hatred they have for each other. Antonio also shows the extent of his love, something Shylock can never match.

**By the end of Act 1** we have met the major characters: Antonio, Shylock, Portia and Bassanio. The great love between Bassanio and Antonio has been demonstrated, as has the hatred between Antonio and Shylock. The pound of flesh bond has been entered into. We learn of the casket bond and of Portia's liking for Bassanio. The foundation for the rest of the action has been laid.

# Self-test (Questions) Act One

## Uncover the plot

Delete two of the three alternatives given, to find the correct plot. Beware possible misconceptions and muddles.

Antonio/Bassanio/Graziano is the Merchant of Venice, who owes lots of money/has money tied up in trade/wants to marry a rich heiress, and goes to the moneylender Tubal/Lancelot Gobbo/Shylock to borrow three thousand pounds/six thousand ducats/three thousand ducats for his friend Stephano/Salanio/Bassanio. It is agreed that if the money is not repaid in six months/three months/one month, the forfeit will be 'thrice three times the value of this bond'/'three chests of gold, silver and lead'/'an equal pound of your fair flesh'.

## Who? What? Where? When?

1 Who will be the 'weeping philosopher' when he grows old?
2 Who would Portia rather shrive her than wive her?
3 Who looks like a fawning publican?
4 Who urges a childlike proof to Antonio?
5 Who cites the Scriptures and how is he described?
6 Who 'caught it, found it, or came by it'? What was it?
7 Who are the 'parcel of wooers'?
8 What is the 'merry sport'?
9 What is 'A stage, where every man must play a part'?
10 What was the childlike proof?
11 What is like a 'villain with a smiling cheek'?
12 What is the Neapolitan prince compared with?
13 What will Tubal do?
14 What would be cursed if Shylock forgave Antonio?
15 What will Antonio supply when he breaks his custom?
16 What has Shylock borne with a patient shrug?
17 What are the 'courtesies' for which Shylock will lend Antonio money?
18 What will the Hebrew 'turn' and what does he 'grow'?

19 Where is a lady richly left?
20 When does Antonio expect to repay the bond?

## Who said that?

1 Who says Antonio 'Is sad to think upon his merchandise?'
2 Who 'speaks an infinite deal of nothing', and who said it?
3 Whose 'body is aweary of this great world'?
4 Who vows to 'die as chaste as Diana' rather than disobey her father's will?
5 Who 'remembers who well, and what is the person worthy of?
6 Who likes not 'fair terms, and a villain's mind'?

## Open quotes

Find the line – and complete the phrase or sentence.
1 'My ventures are not...'
2 'To buy his favour,...'
3 'If to do were as easy as to know...'
4 'I will feed fat...'

## Prove it!

Find a quote from the text that could be used to back up each of the following statements.
1 Shylock hates Antonio.
2 Portia likes Bassanio.
3 Antonio is not sad because of business worries.

## On the other hand

Find a quote from the text that could be used to argue against the following statements.
1 Shylock hates Antonio because Antonio is a Christian.
2 Shylock is fairly liberal in his views: he says he will buy, sell, talk and walk with Bassanio (or Christians generally).

# Self-test (Answers) Act One

## Uncover the plot

Antonio is the Merchant of Venice, who has money tied up in trade, and goes to the moneylender Shylock to borrow three thousand ducats for his friend Bassanio. It is agreed that if the money is not repaid in three months, the forfeit will be 'an equal pound of your fair flesh'.

## Who? What? Where? When?

1 County Palatine 1,2
2 Prince of Morocco 1,2
3 Antonio 1,3
4 Bassanio 1,1
5 Shylock, the devil 1,3
6 Antonio. Sadness 1,1
7 Falconbridge, Monsieur le Bon, County Palatine, etc. 1,2
8 The forfeit of a pound of flesh 1,3
9 The world 1,1
10 Shoot an arrow in the same direction as the one lost, to find both 1,1
11 'An evil soul' 1,3
12 A colt 1,2
13 Lend Shylock the money for Bassanio 1,3
14 His tribe 1,3
15 'The ripe wants of my friend' (Bassanio) 1,3
16 Antonio criticising him for lending money at interest 1,3
17 Spitting on him, cursing him, calling him a dog 1,3
18 Christian, kind 1,3
19 Belmont 1,1
20 A month before it expires 1,3

## Who said that?

1 Salerio 1,1
2 Gratiano, Bassanio 1,1
3 Portia 1,2
4 Portia 1,2
5 Portia remembers Bassanio as being worthy of praise 1,2
6 Bassanio 1,3

## Open quotes

1 'My ventures are not in one bottom trusted, nor to one place.' 1,1
2 'To buy his favour, I extend this friendship.' 1,3
3 'If to do were as easy as to know what were good to do, chapels had been churches, and poor men's cottages princes' palaces.' 1,2
4 'I will feed fat the ancient grudge I bear him.' 1,3

## Prove it!

1 'I hate him for he is a Christian...the ancient grudge I bear him.' 1,3
2 'I remember him well, and I remember him worthy of thy praise.' 1,2
3 'Therefore my merchandise makes me not sad.' 1,1

## On the other hand

1 '...But more for that in low simplicity/He lends out money gratis and brings down/The rate of usance here with us in Venice.' 1,3
2 '...but I will not eat with you, drink with you, nor pray with you.' 1,3

26

## Act 2 Scene 1

*Morocco declares his love for Portia and agrees to abide by the terms of her father's will. If he chooses incorrectly he must leave Belmont immediately and seek to marry another.*

### The Prince of Morocco arrives

*Portia*

Appearance and reality are central to the casket bond. The very first words of the Prince of Morocco ask that he should not be 'misliked' for his colour. He declares his blood is redder than that of any man from a northern climate.

Portia, in response, makes it known that she has no real choice in the matter of what he does, but that he is as good as any she has looked on so far. We know her opinion of the suitors so far and therefore recognise that she is not overjoyed at the prospect of the Prince choosing correctly. Her comment that her father had 'scanted (restricted) me, and hedged me by his wit' suggests she has carefully considered the conditions of the will and has decided they are watertight. She will not break the conditions of this or any other agreement.

### The casket bond forfeit

*The casket test*

As with the bond between Shylock and Antonio, there is a forfeit if the incorrect casket is chosen. However, this is Belmont, a place where love and music hold sway, and the forfeit reflects this fact. Should the wrong casket be chosen, the suitor may never 'speak to lady afterward in way of marriage'. A hard condition but, within the context of the play, one that emphasises the importance of love and the fact that a loving relationship should not be entered into lightly. One must be prepared to venture all for love, just as Antonio has done for his friend Bassanio.

> When the action of the play moves to **Belmont** the main concerns are love and happiness.
>
> **The Prince of Morocco** shows himself to be proud, arrogant and self-centred. He is affected more by outward appearance than inner worth.

## Act 2 Scene 2

*A scene that derives comedy from the grand and pompous language of the Prince of Morocco, introduces some comparisons between Shylock and Bassanio as masters for Launcelot Gobbo, shows again the difference between appearance and reality, suggests that in the end 'truth will out', with the implication that eventually all the plots will find their fruition, and finally gives another example of friendship when Bassanio allows Gratiano to accompany him to Belmont.*

### Launcelot wants a new master

The Jew and the devil would have been synonymous to Elizabethans, so Launcelot's comic soliloquy at the start of the scene presents a 'difficult' decision for him – if he stays in Shylock's service, he stays with 'the devil'; if he obeys the 'fiend' (the devil) and goes to Bassanio, he will offend just the same. The reality is that he has no choice. If Bassanio will have him as a servant then he will join him. Here starts the process by which Shylock will gradually be stripped of all he has: servant, daughter, wealth, religion.

*Shylock*

### Confusions – appearance and reality

Old Gobbo cannot recognise his own son and Launcelot disguises the truth from him for a short while. The confusion between the correct use of various words: infection, defect, impertinent, etc. reflects Shylock's own misuse of the words 'good', 'favour' and 'friendship'. These distortions also bring to mind Antonio's confusion over the Jew's 'kindness'.

### Bassanio and Gratiano prepare for Belmont

You will recall Bassanio's description of Gratiano in the first scene of Act 1 ('speaks an infinite deal of nothing...'). Here he accuses him of being 'too wild, too rude and bold of voice', yet he allows Gratiano to travel to Belmont with him. Given the importance and delicate nature of Bassanio's visit to Belmont and the amount it has cost his friend Antonio , one might wonder at the sense of allowing a person of such 'wild behaviour' to accompany him. What it does underline is the strength of the bonds of friendship and love that these Venetians have for each other. Cold calculations of profit and gain do not enter into the matter when friendship is at stake.

*Bassanio*

Love versus
greed

---

**Bassanio** takes a risk by allowing the 'wild, rude and bold of voice' Gratiano to accompany him on such a delicate mission, especially in view of the high stakes he and Antonio have at risk. It says much for the bonds of friendship – or perhaps Bassanio undervalues the risk involved: his profligate use of Antonio's money in the past showed little sense.

**The Gobbos** provide some light relief.

# Act 2 Scene 3

*The action returns to Venice and Shylock's household. Jessica gives a letter to Launcelot, for Lorenzo. She regrets that she is Shylock's daughter and looks forward to eloping with Lorenzo.*

### Jessica talks of life at home with Shylock

The elopement

Jessica acquaints us with her unhappiness at home. The fact that Shylock is a lone figure in the play is underlined by the fact that even his own daughter is ashamed of him – not a normal circumstance in any household, Jewish or not.

Again reference is made to changing religion; ironically, both Jessica and Shylock will become Christians, but for very different reasons.

The reference to Lorenzo indicates that another part of this tale is about to be disclosed.

# Act 2 Scene 4

*Lorenzo, Gratiano, Solanio and Salerio are preparing for the masque being held by Bassanio. Launcelot arrives with Jessica's message and Lorenzo promises he will not fail her. He tells Gratiano of his plans.*

### Lorenzo plots Jessica's elopement

The elopement

Jessica is to leave her father's house disguised as a page. She will also take his gold and jewels. Shylock should have been able to give his daughter his love and his wealth. The one thing that cannot be stolen by his daughter, which is worth far more than material things, he does not give her at all – his love. His wealth, which he values above all, she steals. It is for you to decide how 'just' you think this is. Thus he is to be left with nothing – except perhaps the prospect of revenge on Antonio.

# Act 2 Scene 5

*Bassanio has sent a letter inviting Shylock to dinner. Shylock is reluctant to go.*

### Shylock leaves Jessica in charge

There is an interesting parallel here. Shylock is to leave Jessica in charge of his house with strict instructions to keep it and his goods secure. Ironically, whilst he is gone she will first take his wealth and then, in disguise, elope with Lorenzo. Later she will, with Lorenzo, be left in charge of Portia's house. But that will be in Belmont, and the only thing that happens there is that Lorenzo and Jessica's love

Shylock

for each other grows – certainly no one's house will be robbed. Shylock's determination to 'go in hate to feed upon the prodigal Christian' reminds us of the prejudice and hate in his character. His account of his dreams makes him slightly comic. Any sympathy the audience might have for him and the fate he will suffer at his daughter's hands is swept away by his own words and attitudes.

Shylock is right to worry about his 'money bags'. He shows his hatred for the Venetians and their music: contrast this to the atmosphere in Belmont. He distrusts the masques and is right to do so, for Lorenzo and friends will come in disguise to take Jessica away.

His concern with profit colours all his actions, as is evidenced by his reference to Lancelot as being 'snail-slow in profit'.

## Act 2 Scene 6

*Jessica, disguised as a boy, elopes with Lorenzo, taking Shylock's money and jewels with her. Antonio arrives to tell Gratiano that Bassanio is departing for Belmont.*

### Jessica elopes and takes Shylock's money and jewellery

The elopement

This is an interesting scene in that we are presented with the uncomfortable knowledge that Jessica, with whom we are surely meant to sympathise, breaks two of the Ten Commandments by which Christians should order their lives: she fails to honour her father and she steals. Against her actions are to be balanced the audience's dislike of Shylock and Jessica's own hatred of him. The light-hearted tone of the scene and the obvious love of Lorenzo for Jessica help us perhaps to consider her actions in a more forgiving light.

Antonio

Note Gratiano's comments on how the outcome of events often belies the original expectations. Perhaps most ominous is his reference to ships that return 'lean, rent, and beggared by the strumpet wind', placing Antonio's risk in the context of Shylock's daughter eloping with a Christian – Shylock's anger may well be vented on Antonio.

### Away to Belmont

Antonio's arrival with the news that the wind has shifted and that Bassanio is about to depart reintroduces the casket bond and moves us smoothly back to Belmont.

# Act 2 Scene 7

*The Prince of Morocco makes his choice from the three caskets. He reads the inscription on each, judges that gold is right and fails. He departs, leaving Portia very relieved.*

### Morocco goes for gold – appearance and reality

**The casket test**

**Love versus greed**

You must be clear about the inscriptions on each casket. Note how they talk of what men 'desire' and 'deserve', and of giving and hazarding all one has. There is a link here between the casket bond and pound of flesh bond. Shylock desires gold but one might consider that eventually he gets what he deserves. Yes, Antonio is a merchant and presumably also pursues gold, but he is also willing to hazard all that he has for something that Shylock presumably would consider worthless and profitless – friendship and love.

The Prince rejects the lead casket. Its appearance disguises, for him, the reality of what it contains. He uses the wrong standards by which to judge it.

### 'All that glisters is not gold'

At first the Prince finds it difficult to choose between the silver and gold caskets. He believes he deserves Portia, but he cannot reconcile the differences in external value between silver and gold. The contrasts in wealth that they represent lead him inexorably towards choosing the appearance of wealth and riches. Note that this is a path that Shylock has followed and which has lost him his wealth and his daughter.

The Prince is as much concerned with his own worth and what he deserves as with the worth of the caskets and what they represent.

**The casket test**

The contents of the gold casket, a skull and a scroll, dramatically highlight the distinction between the appearance of the casket and the reality of what was inside: 'Gilded tombs do worms infold' vividly reflects the Biblical image of whited sepulchres, ornate tombs which contain bones and decay.

# Act 2 Scene 8

*Solanio and Salerio derive amusement from discussing Shylock's public woe at his daughter's elopement and the theft of his money and jewels. Antonio's ships may be lost and they worry that Shylock's grief may be taken out on Antonio.*

## A return to Venice

From the Prince of Morocco's disappointment caused by his choice of the gold that 'glisters' we move swiftly back to Venice and hear of Shylock's utter dismay at the loss of his gold and jewels: the Jew's home is as empty of wealth as Morocco's casket was of Portia.

**The elopement**

Solanio's impersonation of Shylock voices his major concerns: his ducats, his jewels, his daughter and justice. Shylock is portrayed as a laughable figure. However, be aware that the cry for his daughter is only a wish to bring her back for retribution; his cry for justice is effectively a cry for revenge.

**Shylock**

## Antonio at risk

Again there is talk of Antonio's ships being at risk and the warning that he should beware Shylock's hatred, else he will be made to pay for the Jew's woe.

## Antonio's love for Bassanio

The description of the parting of Bassanio and Antonio again highlights their love and friendship for each other and the extent to which Antonio is prepared to sacrifice his wealth and well-being for Bassanio: 'I think he only loves the world for him.' He even goes so far as to counsel Bassanio not to worry about the time it may take to win Portia's hand. This part of the scene again provides a strong contrast between the concerns of Shylock and Antonio. For the former it is ducats and jewels; for the latter, love for a friend.

The next communication between Antonio and Bassanio will be Antonio's letter asking that he might see his friend again before he forfeits his life for Bassanio's sake.

**Antonio**

**Love versus greed**

# Act 2 Scene 9

*The Prince of Arragon chooses the silver casket and fails to win Portia's hand. A messenger arrives to announce that Bassanio has come to choose between the caskets. Portia and Nerissa hope that he will succeed.*

## The Prince of Arragon

**The casket test**

The price of failure to choose the correct casket is again spelled out: never to tell which casket was chosen, never to pursue any maid for marriage, and to depart from Belmont immediately.

The Prince dismisses the lead casket with hardly a second glance. Reading the warning on the lead casket that he must be prepared to 'give and hazard all he hath', the Prince cannot bring himself to consider such a sacrifice for 'base lead'. Having arrogantly dismissed the lead casket because of its apparent low worth, he ironically dismisses the gold because the 'fool multitude' would 'choose by show' – the very fault he demonstrated when rejecting the lead casket. It demonstrates both his low opinion of others and the high opinion he holds of himself.

## Arragon chooses silver

'I will assume desert' is Arragon's reason for choosing silver. In doing so, he shows an arrogance of spirit and self-love which contradicts everything Belmont stands for. It parallels Shylock's mean spirit and his short-sighted 'love' for his jewels, his ducats, his daughter.

The contents of the casket are a fool's head and a scroll. The scroll's words say that his 'desert' is a mere shadow, something 'silvered' but only overlaid, not solid. He was a fool and the fool's head is appropriate for a person of such vanity.

## Bassanio arrives at Belmont

The news that Bassanio has arrived links the worlds of Belmont and Venice. Portia comments a little warily on the enthusiasm with which his arrival is announced, but Nerissa seems to be sure of what she wants: 'Bassanio, lord Love, if thy will it be!'

---

By the end of Act 2, many of the essential elements are in place:

- The bond of friendship between Antonio and Bassanio has been established
- The pound of flesh bond between Antonio and Shylock has been entered into
- Antonio's ships are reported to be in danger
- Bassanio's wish to marry Portia has put Antonio's life in danger, but their marriage will eventually save his live
- Shylock's reasons for entering into the bond with Antonio are greed and malice

- Shylock's daughter rejects him and his religion, and steals his money and jewels

- Portia, evidently intelligent and witty, submits to her father's will and abides by his decrees as to how she should find a husband

Act 2 builds on the first Act. **In Venice**, Shylock's misfortunes begin: Launcelot, his servant, leaves him; his daughter elopes and steals ducats and jewels from him; Shylock bemoans his fate in public and becomes a figure of fun; we hear details of his hatred for Christians. News arrives that Antonio's ships are lost at sea. Shylock's misfortunes concentrate his mind on harming Antonio.

**In Belmont**, the casket bond is developed. Morocco and Arragon, respectively, choose the gold and silver caskets, and fail. News of Bassanio's arrival suggests the casket bond may soon be settled.

# Self-test (Questions) Act Two

## Uncover the plot

Delete two of the three alternatives given, to find the correct plot. Beware possible misconceptions and muddles.

In Belmont/Venice/Morocco, the casket bond proceeds: with two suitors already rejected, news comes that the Prince of Morocco/Bassanio/Prince of Aragon is at Portia's gate. Meanwhile, Shylock is left bewailing the loss of 'my servant and my daughter'/'my daughter and my jewels'/'my ducats and my daughter'. His servant Launcelot/Lorenzo/Leonardo has left him for Bassanio, and his daughter Nerissa/Jessica/Portia has eloped with Lorenzo – and the treasure. There is, however, some news that will gladden Shylock's heart: 'she hath the stones upon her and the ducats'/'all that glisters is not gold'/'there miscarried/A vessel of our country richly fraught'.

## Who? What? Where? Why?

1 Who is 'a huge feeder/Snail slow in profit'?
2 Who is asked 'to allay with some cold drops of modesty/Thy skipping spirit', and by whom?
3 What is Jessica to wear for her elopement, and what role will she play?
4 What three promises attend the choice of the wrong casket?
5 What does Shylock cry for in the streets?
6 Where did Shylock first go when he discovered his loss?
7 Where was Shylock while Jessica escaped his house?
8 Why does Shylock have a sense of 'ill a-brewing'?
9 Why is Shylock particularly happy to let Lorenzo go to Bassanio's household?
10 Why does the Prince of Morocco fear Portia will 'mislike' him?

## Who said that?

1 Who is urged to 'stay the very riping of the time', where, for what, and by whom?
2 Who says: 'I think he only loves the world for him' – and who are the lover and beloved?
3 Who calls whom 'wise, fair and true'?
4 Who says: 'Our house is hell; and thou, a merry devil, /Didst rob it of some taste of tediousness', and of whom?
5 Who says: 'I'll then nor give nor hazard aught for lead'?

## Open quotes

Find the line – and complete the phrase or sentence.
1 'The boy was the very staff...'
2 'And if my fortune be not crost...'
3 'But yet I'll go in hate...'
4 'In terms of choice, I am not solely led...'

## Prove it!

Find a quote from the text that could be used to back up each of the following statements.
1 Portia feels she has no choice in the selection of her future husband.
2 Jessica is torn between duty and shame with regard to her father.

## On the other hand

Find THREE quotes from the text that could be used to argue against the following statement: each from a different speaker!
1 Jessica is an Elizabethan stereotype of a Jewess, in the same mould as Shylock himself.

## Make the connection

Join up the elements of the casket bond that 'suit' each other!

| 3 caskets | 3 inscriptions | 3 prizes | 2 messages | 2 unsuccessful suitors |
|-----------|----------------|----------|------------|------------------------|
| Gold | 'Who chooseth me, shall get as much as he deserves' | Portrait of Portia, and her hand in marriage | 'All that glisters is not gold.../Gilded tombs do worms infold' | ...... |
| Silver | 'Who chooseth me, must give and hazard all he hath' | Scroll and a portrait of 'a blinking idiot' | ...... | Morocco |
| Lead | 'Who chooseth me, shall gain what many men desire' | Scroll and skull | 'Some there be that shadows kiss,/ Such have but a shadow's bliss' | Arragon |

# Self-test (Answers) Act Two

## Uncover the plot

In Belmont the casket bond proceeds: with two suitors already rejected, news comes that Bassanio is at Portia's gate. Meanwhile, Shylock is left bewailing the loss of 'my ducats and my daughter'. His servant Launcelot has left him for Bassanio, and his daughter Jessica has eloped with Lorenzo – and the treasure. There is, however, some news that will gladden Shylock's heart: 'there miscarried/A vessel of our country richly fraught'.

## Who? What? Where? Why?

1 Launcelot 2,5
2 Gratiano, by Bassanio 2,2
3 Boy's clothes, torch bearer 2,4
4 1: 'Never to unfold to any one/Which casket 'twas I chose'
   2: 'Never to speak to a lady afterward/In way of marriage'
   3: 'Immediately to leave you and be gone' 2,9
5 Justice, law, ducats, daughter, jewels 2,8
6 With the Duke, to search Bassanio's ship 2,8
7 At dinner with Bassanio 2,4
8 Because he has dreamed of money bags 2,5
9 Because he 'would have him help to waste/His borrowed purse.' 2,5
10 Because of his colour, or 'complexion' 2,1

## Who said that?

1 Bassanio, in Belmont, for courtship, by Antonio 2,8
2 Solanio, Antonio and Bassanio 2,8
3 Lorenzo, of Jessica 2,6
4 Jessica, of Launcelot 2,3
5 Prince of Morocco 2,7

## Open quotes

1 'The boy was the very staff of my age, my very prop.' (Old Gobbo of Launcelot 2,2)

2 'And if my fortune be not crost', I have a father, you a daughter, lost.' (Jessica 2,5)
3 'But yet I'll go in hate to feed upon/The prodigal Christian.' (Shylock 2,3)
4 'In terms of choice, I am not solely led/By nice direction of a maiden's eye' (Portia 2,1)

## Prove it!

1 'Besides, the lott'ry of my destiny/Bars me the right of voluntary choosing.' 2,1
2 'Alack, what heinous sin it is in me/To be ashamed to be my father's child.' 2,3

## On the other hand

1 'Though I am a daughter to his blood/I am not to his manners.' (Jessica 2,3)
2 'If e'er the Jew her father came to heaven/It will be for his gentle daughter's sake.' (Lorenzo 2,4)
3 'Now, by my hood, a gentle, and no Jew.' (Gratiano 2,4)

## Make the connection

3 caskets    3 inscriptions    3 prizes    2 messages    2 unsuccessful suitors

Gold   'Who chooseth me, shall get as much as he deserves'   Portrait of Portia, and her hand in marriage   'All that glisters is not gold.../Gilded tombs do worms infold'   ......

Silver   'Who chooseth me, must give and hazard all he hath'   Scroll and a portrait of 'a blinking idiot'   ......   Morocco

Lead   'Who chooseth me, shall gain what many men desire'   Scroll and skull   'Some there be that shadows kiss./Such have but a shadow's bliss'   Arragon

# Act 3 Scene 1

*The three months of the flesh bond are almost up. Solanio and Salerio discuss the likelihood of Antonio's ships being lost. Shylock arrives and bemoans his losses. In this famous speech, he suggests that Jews are the same as Christians and may therefore claim revenge when they are wronged. To him, this justifies his hatred for Antonio. Tubal gives Shylock the bad news about how Jessica is spending his money, and then the good news that Antonio's ships are lost.*

## News of Antonio's ships

The Act opens in Venice with the news that one of Antonio's ships is reported to have been sunk. Hot on the heels of this news, Shylock enters.

His concern that his daughter has fled is a source of entertainment to Salerio and Solanio and they draw a clear distinction between Shylock and his daughter. She may have been born to him and be of his race but in reality she is no more akin to him than is Portia.

The elopement

## 'If you prick us, do we not bleed?'

Shylock

In this well-known speech, Shylock first lists the wrongs that he says Antonio has done him, and then he proceeds to consider the similarities between Christians and Jews – they are both human with the same 'organs, dimensions, senses, affections, passions…': 'If you prick us, do we not bleed?'

We might agree with Shylock's sentiments and accept that he has just cause to hate Antonio. However, the next stage of his argument, that being like a Christian he can call for revenge, runs completely counter to the whole tenor of a major theme of the play – mercy versus justice. To Shylock, the latter is just another word for revenge. This speech helps to prepare the audience for Shylock's virulent pursuit of the bond's forfeit.

## Shylock 'bleeds', hearing of his own losses

Any sympathy the audience might have for Shylock as a result of his impassioned speech quickly evaporates as they listen to him rail against his daughter. His only concerns are for his ducats, his jewels and now more ominously, his revenge.

Tubal's report that one of Antonio's ships has been sunk off the coast of Tripoli is greeted by Shylock with great happiness. Along with everyone else, Tubal seems to delight in teasing Shylock, emphasising his aloneness. Here, he reminds him that Jessica is spending his money, but then balances that bad news by talking about various of Antonio's creditors, who worry they will not be paid. Then, swiftly, he tells of a ring which Jessica has sold, one given Shylock by his wife; but then, again, he reassures Shylock that 'Antonio is certainly undone'.

By the end of the scene any sympathy that Shylock might have gained is effectively negated by the spectacle of him being wickedly manipulated by Tubal, showing him at his worst. Note that throughout this scene Shylock's only concern is for himself: any suggestion of his suffering for or because of the Jewish race has been abandoned.

*Shylock*

### Shylock sets 'justice' in motion

His final words to Tubal 'were he (Antonio) out of Venice, I can make what merchandise I will' summarise his purpose in pursuing 'justice' against Antonio; and of making profit through revenge.

> The pound of flesh bond develops: Antonio's ships are reported lost, the three months are up, and the time is ripe for Shylock to take his revenge.

# Act 3 Scene 2

*Bassanio wins Portia's hand by choosing the lead casket, rejecting the outward show of the silver and gold caskets. Inside he finds a picture of Portia and a verse confirming he has made the right choice. Gratiano and Nerissa announce they are also in love. Rings are given by the women to bind their lovers to them. News of Antonio's failure to pay the bond arrives. Portia offers to pay the 3000 ducats, even 36 000 if need be. Bassanio departs for Venice.*

### Portia wants Bassanio to delay choosing a casket

Portia's plea to Bassanio 'I pray you, tarry: pause a day or two... I would detain you here some month or two' shows how much she wishes him to be successful and that she is worried that he might choose the wrong casket.

'One half of me is yours...' the concept of giving totally is repeated here. Portia loves Bassanio, but her desire for him will not drive her to break the bond imposed by her father, even

*Portia*

though she might lose Bassanio because of it. Her determination to live within the letter of the law is demonstrated later in the play when she declines Bassanio's invitation at the trial: 'To do a great right, do a little wrong.' Her answer, '...many an error by the same sample will rush into the state', shows how clearly she sees the evil consequences which may follow such an action. Note how her attitude parallels that of Antonio, who shows a similar determination to be bound by the law, regardless of the consequences for himself, when he is called upon to honour the pound of flesh bond.

**The casket test**

Portia has faith in her father's will. She realises that if Bassanio loves her he will not be distracted by the appearances of the caskets as were her other suitors.

### 'Let music sound'

Portia commands that music be played whilst Bassanio makes his choice. Belmont is a place of love, friendship and happiness, where Portia will find her husband. It is fitting that music should accompany Bassanio's choice – her command is in striking contrast to Shylock's response to music in Act 2 Scene 5: 'the vile squealing'.

### Appearance and reality

'So may the outward shows be least themselves:
The world is still deceived with ornament.
In law, what plea so tainted and corrupt,
But, being season'd with a gracious voice,
Obscures the show of evil?'

In these five lines, Bassanio encapsulates major elements of the play. The appearance of things has little to do with their reality and so Bassanio will not be deceived by the worth of the metals from which the caskets are made. This quotation also has relevance for Shylock's desire for 'justice' which is really a quest first for revenge, and then for profit once Antonio is dead. Again, the 'plea so tainted and corrupt' aptly describes Shylock's 'do we not bleed...' speech, and looks forward to Shylock's plea for justice and law at Antonio's trial.

### No gold or silver for Bassanio

Bassanio devotes some time to exploring the contradictions between appearance and reality, and his final words, 'The seeming truth which cunning times put on/ To entrap the wisest' lead logically and correctly to his rejection of the gold and silver caskets.

**The casket test**

His correct choice of the lead casket is greeted with joy by Portia and they both talk of their willingness to give all to each other and of their unworthiness to receive each other's love.

> The casket bond has been happily resolved, and the purpose of the flesh bond therefore achieved. It now remains for the forfeit to be paid.

### Another bond – rings

'I give them with this ring...' The giving of the ring symbolises all of Portia's possessions, given freely to Bassanio. However, as with all bonds there is a forfeit to be paid if it is broken. Here in Belmont, the bond and forfeit are not based on

The ring bond

money but on love and giving. However, with the resolution of the casket bond, the creation of this new bond serves to remind us that another has yet to run its course – the pound of flesh bond.

Bassanio's friendship for Gratiano seems to have had good effect. The marriage between Gratiano and Nerissa, Portia's companion, is announced – surely another lesson in how true love and friendship, the willingness to give all, brings its own reward. In contrast, Shylock will lose all.

### Lorenzo and Jessica join the happy couples

The elopement

The arrival of the party from Venice completes the group of happy lovers. However, the happiness is soon overshadowed by other news from Venice.

Lorenzo's part in the play is very small. He provides the means for Jessica's elopement and causes Shylock distress in taking his daughter, jewels and money from him.

### A letter from Antonio

Bassanio describes to Portia the debt he owes Antonio and the trouble his friend is now in. The suggestions made in previous scenes that Antonio's ships might be at risk, have come true. All his ventures have failed. Worse news is related by Salerio.

### Shylock's vow

The pound of flesh bond

Shylock has demanded justice. He will not have repayment of the money due to him. As Antonio has not paid on time, Shylock is demanding payment of the forfeit. He demands justice and his bond: 'he would rather have Antonio's flesh / Than twenty times the value of the sum / That he (Antonio) did owe him.'

The realities of Shylock's plotting and desires are now disclosed. All his fine words, which Bassanio saw through, are now shown for what they really were: a ploy to get Antonio within his grasp.

### Portia offers help

Love versus greed

Portia swiftly supports Bassanio's desire to help his friend by placing all her wealth at his disposal, and suggests he depart for Venice as soon as they are married. Her love for Bassanio knows no limits in what she is prepared to do for him. Similarly, Antonio's letter shows generosity of spirit to Bassanio.

His only wish is that he should see Bassanio before his (Antonio's) death.

Note that Portia's words 'Pay him six thousand... Double six thousand and then treble that' amounts to 36 000 ducats. Later, in Act 4, Shylock will reject this same amount without it actually being offered. He will also reject the suggestion from Portia that he must show mercy if Antonio is to live.

# Act 3 Scene 3

*Antonio's makes a last, useless plea to Shylock. Shylock rejects it, demanding the forfeit of the bond. Antonio wishes only that he may see Bassanio before he dies.*

Antonio

### Shylock demands justice

'Tell me not of mercy' introduces a concept that Shylock wants nothing to do with. Ironically, his determination to have nothing to do with mercy will be at the root of his downfall. He sets his mind against it here, and continues to do so at the trial. His bond and justice are what Shylock is determined to have. He senses that he has Antonio at his mercy at last, but there is no mercy for Antonio in Shylock's heart.

### The law must take its course

Antonio recognises that the Duke of Venice cannot deny the course of law. To do so would destroy the credibility of Venice as a trading state. Antonio's only concern now is to see Bassanio so that he might 'see me pay his debt'. Antonio will willingly sacrifice his life for his friend. Contrast this with Shylock's repeated 'I'll have my bond'.

# Act 3 Scene 4

*Portia leaves her house to go to a monastery. Lorenzo and Jessica are to be left in charge of Portia's house – no likelihood here of theft or elopement! Really, Portia and Nerissa are to travel to Venice disguised as lawyer and clerk, to defend Antonio.*

Portia knows that she is capable of disguising and passing herself off as a young, bragging lawyer: 'I have within my mind/A thousand raw tricks'.

## Act 3 Scene 5

*Jessica, Lorenzo and Launcelot are at Belmont.*

The final scene of Act 3 again raises the problems caused by Jessica's elopement and her theft of Shylock's money and jewels. Jessica's theft from her father ought to bring criticism from us, but doesn't. In a sense she is no longer his daughter, as his actions and attitudes have reduced his moral and parental authority. In stealing from her father it could be said that Jessica is merely taking her birthright and, in doing so, adds to the comedy of Shylock's position.

**The elopement**

Her praise of Portia is freely and eloquently given. The scene ends on a light note and we are ready for the tensions of the trial.

---

**By the end of Act 3** the casket bond has been resolved, and the ring bond has been entered into by Bassanio and Gratiano.

**Portia** shows herself determined to help her husband's friend.

**Shylock and Antonio** have confronted each other for the last time, outside the court.

**Shylock** is determined to exact his forfeit and Antonio prepares to die, wishing only to see Bassanio before he does.

**Jessica and Lorenzo** have reached the safety of Belmont.

The way is clear for the trial.

---

## Uncover the plot

Delete two of the three alternatives given, to find the correct plot. Beware possible misconceptions and muddles.

On the Rialto, Antonio's/Bassanio's/Tubal's ship is reported wrecked: Shylock hears the good news 'from Salerio/Solanio/Tubal and resolves to 'have another bad match'/'have the heart of him'/'have hands, organs, dimensions, senses....'. In Belmont, Bassanio chooses the gold/silver/lead casket, and wins Portia – while Gratiano/Lorenzo/Salerio declares his love for Nerissa. Salerio appears with a letter from Antonio/Shylock/the Duke. Portia offers to pay 3,000/6,000/36 000 ducats to cancel Antonio's bond and sends Bassanio to his friend – meanwhile planning to 'live in prayer and contemplation'/go disguised to Venice/pay the petty debt 20 times over'. In Venice, Antonio resigns himself to death, if he can only have revenge on Shylock/pay back his debt/ see Bassanio once more. Left in Belmont, Jessica and Launcelot/Nerissa/Lorenzo start their life together.

## Who? What? Where? Why?

1 Who are the 'Jasons', and what 'fleece' have they won?
2 Who is given the 'husbandry and manage' of Portia's house?
3 Who is it 'in whom/The ancient Roman honour more appears/Than any that draws breath in Italy'?
4 What does Portia 'give...with this ring'?
5 What is more different than jet and ivory?
6 What is Shylock's 'loss upon loss'?
7 Where are Nerissa and Portia supposed to await their husbands' return?
8 Who is Portia's cousin, where does he live, and what does she ask him for?
9 Why is Portia inclined to delay the choice of caskets?
10 Why does Antonio think Shylock hates him?

## Who said that?

1 Who said: 'If we are like you in the rest, we will resemble you in that'? Who is 'we' and 'you', and what are 'the rest' and 'that'?
2 Who says: 'In measure rain thy joy, scant this excess!'
3 Who says: 'Tell me not of mercy, and to whom?

4 Who says: 'Having such a blessing in his lady,/He finds the joys of heaven here on earth' and of whom?
5 Who says: 'But when this ring/Parts from this finger, then parts life from hence'?

## Open quotes

Find the line – and complete the phrase or sentence.
1 'You that choose not by the view....'
2 'For never shall you lie by Portia's side....'
3 'If you prick us...If you tickle us...If you poison us...If you wrong us....'
4 'In law, what plea so tainted and corrupt....'

## Prove it!

Find THREE quotes from the text that could be used to back up the following statement.
1 Shylock is determined to kill Antonio.

## On the other hand

Find a quote from the text that could be used to argue against the following statements.
1 Shylock, at heart, loves his daughter more than his treasure.
2 Shylock's desire for revenge is presented as an un-Christian trait.

## There's good news...and bad news...

Find the words of hope which match the words of despair – or vice versa.

| POSITIVE | NEGATIVE |
|---|---|
| 'Your daughter spent in Genoa, as I heard, in one night, four score ducats.' | |
| 'He hath disgrac'd me and hind'red me half a million.' | |
| | 'He may win.../...then music is/Even as the flourish...' |
| | 'Not sick, my lord, unless it be in mind.' |
| | 'The Duke/Will never grant this forfeiture to hold.' |
| 'You are damned both by father and mother!' | |

# Self-test (Answers) Act Three

## Uncover the plot

On the Rialto, Antonio's ship is reported wrecked. Shylock hears the 'good news' from Tubal and resolves to 'have the heart of him'. In Belmont, Bassanio chooses the lead casket and wins Portia – while Gratiano declares his love for Nerissa. Salerio appears with a letter from Antonio. Portia offers to pay 36 000 ducats to cancel Antonio's bond and sends Bassanio to his friend – meanwhile planning to go disguised to Venice. In Venice, Antonio resigns himself to death, if he can only see Bassanio once more. Left in Belmont, Jessica and Lorenzo start their life together.

## Who? What? Where? Why?

1   Bassanio and Gratiano, Portia and Nerissa 3,2
2   Lorenzo and Jessica 3,4
3   Antonio 3,2
4   House, servants and self 3,2
5   Shylock's flesh and Jessica's 3,1
6   The treasure 'stolen' by his daughter – plus more money 'spent in the search' for them 3,1
7   At a monastery two miles away from Portia's house in Belmont 3,4
8   Doctor Bellario, Padua, 'notes and garments' 3,4
9   Because she is afraid Bassanio will fail 3,2
10  Because he has 'deliver'd' many debtors from Shylock's clutches 3,3

## Who said that?

1   Shylock; Jews and Christians; 'hands, organs, dimensions, senses', etc. and desire for revenge 3,1
2   Portia 3,2
3   Shylock, to the gaoler/Antonio 3,3
4   Jessica, of Portia 3,5
5   Bassanio 3,2

## Open quotes

1   'You that choose not by the view/Chance as fair and choose as true!' 3,2
2   'For never shall you lie by Portia's side,/With an unquiet soul.' 3,2
3   'If you prick us, do we not bleed? If you tickle us, do we not laugh? If you poison us, do we not die? And if you wrong us, shall we not avenge?' 3,1
4   'In law, what plea so tainted and corrupt/But being season'd with a gracious voice,/Obscures the show of evil?' 3,2

## Prove it!

1   'I have sworn an oath that I will have my bond.' 3,3
2   'But none can drive him from the envious plea,/Of forfeiture, of justice and his bond.' 3,2
3   '...he would rather have Antonio's flesh/Then twenty times the value of the sum.' 3,2

## There's good news...and bad news...

## On the other hand

1   'I would my daughter were dead at my foot, and the jewels in her ear.' 3,1
2   'The villainy you teach me I will execute.' 3,1

| POSITIVE | NEGATIVE |
|---|---|
| 'Your daughter spent in Genoa, as I heard, in one night, four score ducats.' | 'Antonio is certainly undone.' (3,1) |
| 'He hath disgrac'd me and hind'red me half a million.' | 'I'll plague him, I'll torture him.' |
| 'If he lose, he makes a swan-like end,/Fading in music' (3,2) | 'He may win,.../...then music is/Even as the flourish...' |
| 'Nor well, unless in mind.' (3,2) | 'Not sick, my lord, unless it be in mind.' |
| 'The Duke cannot deny the course of law.' (3,3) | 'The Duke/Will never grant this forfeiture to hold.' |
| 'You are damned both by father and mother!' | 'I shall be saved by my husband.' (3,5) |

# Act 4 Scene 1

*The trial scene. Antonio is brought to trial so that Shylock may claim the forfeit of his bond. He rejects pleas for mercy from the Duke and demands the law. Portia, disguised as a lawyer, judges that Shylock must be merciful if Antonio is to live. Shylock demands the law, and gets it. For threatening the life of a Venetian he loses all he has and his life is at the mercy of the Duke.*

## The Duke's opinion of Shylock

Shylock

The Duke's greeting for Antonio is warm, but he damns Shylock with great forcefulness, calling him 'A stony adversary, an inhuman wretch,/Uncapable of pity, void and empty/From any dram of mercy.' Hardly, in modern eyes, a suitable judge to try this case. However, Shylock has already lost our pity and the Duke's words merely serve to confirm the audience's views, summarising the character of Shylock as we have come to know him.

Antonio

Antonio tells the Duke that he accepts the verdict of the law and will oppose Shylock's fury with patience and a 'quietness of spirit'. This points to his noble nature, already demonstrated in the sacrifices he has made for Bassanio and voiced in his letter where his last wish is to see Bassanio before dying.

Notwithstanding his jaundiced view of Shylock, the Duke tries to reason with him, and attempts to play upon feelings of compassion and mercy for a fellow human being. This is an interesting parallel with Shylock's own 'If you prick me ...' speech. There, Shylock tried to gain our sympathy for his cause by appealing to the common fellowship and feelings of man. Here, the Duke tries a similar plea, but it falls on deaf ears.

Love versus greed

The import of Shylock's long response to the Duke is that he would rather have the pound of flesh than the money because it 'humours' him, and the only reason he can give is a 'lodged hate and a certain loathing' he has for Antonio. These comparatively weak responses contrast strongly with the virulence of the hatred and desire for revenge he has previously expressed for Antonio. And do not forget the profit that Shylock expects to gain when Antonio and the nil rate of interest he charges are removed from Venice.

Antonio

Antonio joins this discussion by stating plainly that he knows Shylock will not forgo his rights to the forfeit. Antonio recognises and accepts the inevitability of the law's judgement and the implacable determination of Shylock to pursue his legal case. He accuses Shylock of having a hard heart – and therefore no capacity for friendship, love or mercy.

Shylock

When Bassanio offers him yet more money, Shylock refuses. He says that even if the six thousand ducats offered were multiplied by six (i.e. 36 000) he would 'not draw them'. It is interesting that, without knowing it, he has here rejected the very amount that Portia said she would be willing to pay. By implication he is already rejecting her, just as he will reject her plea for mercy.

### 'How shalt thou hope for mercy...?'

Mercy versus justice

The Duke taxes him with the question, 'How shalt thou hope for mercy, rendering none?' and in doing so prepares us for the time when the court and its officers will show Shylock no mercy. Shylock here effectively seals his own fate by rejecting mercy and desiring only the law. His accusation, in his own defence, that the Venetians treat their slaves without compassion, regarding them as property to do with as they will, perhaps makes us a little uneasy. Do be aware that twentieth-century views regarding slavery do not sit easily with Elizabethan attitudes. But, whatever Shylock's justification for his actions, he could still have been merciful. Instead, he chooses the law and his rights.

Love versus greed

And there we have an end to it, as far as Shylock and Antonio are concerned. Hatred, revenge and profit must have their way. But we have yet to see the influence of Belmont, of friendship and love, of mercy, and of Portia the lawyer.

However, before Portia, disguised as a young lawyer, can appear, Bassanio offers to lay down his own life for Antonio, a sacrifice as great as Antonio is prepared to make for him.

### Shylock sharpens his knife

Shylock

Following hard on the heels of Antonio's and Bassanio's eloquent willingness to die for each other, we have the almost obscene picture of Shylock whetting (sharpening) his knife, ready and anxious to cut into Antonio's flesh. The intervention of Gratiano who, in typical robust fashion, roundly curses Shylock and accuses him of being 'wolvish, bloody, starved and ravenous', provides a short respite, allowing for Portia, disguised as Balthasar, a young lawyer from Padua, to be introduced.

---

Pleas from the Duke for mercy, offers from Bassanio of more money and curses from Gratiano all fail to move Shylock from his purpose. He has one, and only one desire, 'I stand here for the law'. The trial must start.

### Portia intervenes – 'then must the Jew be merciful'

The brief formalities of identifying Shylock and Antonio, and of confirming their acknowledgement of the bond being over, Portia confirms the rule of Venetian law and declares that for Antonio to escape death, the Jew must be merciful.

Note how she immediately reflects the Duke's plea to Shylock to be merciful. We are, of course, already aware of Shylock's response to the Duke on this count, and are not surprised when Shylock asks under what compulsion must he be merciful.

**Mercy versus justice**

### 'The quality of mercy is not strained'

Perhaps the most famous of the speeches from this play, Portia's powerful exposition of the quality and reason for mercy makes little impression on Shylock.

### 'It blesseth him that gives and him that takes'

– much like the qualities of friendship and love so amply demonstrated by Antonio, Bassanio, Portia and their friends. However, mercy transcends all earthly qualities and is an 'attribute to God himself'.

### 'mercy seasons justice'

Justice is what Shylock demands. Portia shows that justice will bring none of us to salvation unless we also have mercy. However, she concludes that if Shylock rejects the plea for mercy then this 'strict court of Venice' must give judgement against Antonio, the merchant of Venice.

When Bassanio pleads with her to bend the laws of Venice: 'To do a great right, do a little wrong', she pointedly refuses because of the precedents such an action would set, which might then lead to even greater wrongs being done in the future. Her response is greeted with glee by Shylock and he charges her 'by the law' to proceed to judgement.

It is at this point that Portia encourages Shylock to show everyone how far he is prepared to go, and the true inhumanity and lack of any mercy which accompanies the deed. Shylock will use his own knife, sharpened in full view of the audience, and will cut the flesh himself. He has brought his own set of scales to weigh the flesh, and is scornful of Portia when she suggests that for humanity's sake he should provide a surgeon to stop the bleeding: 'Is it so nominated in the bond?' He will have his bond, and nothing else.

**The pound of flesh bond**

### Antonio prepares to die

For a brief moment, Antonio and Bassanio reaffirm their love and friendship for each other. A dignified and touching scene, particularly in contrast to the

bloodthirsty and homicidal attitude of Shylock.

The audience is reminded of the true relationships between the characters in this scene, when both Portia and Nerissa react to Bassanio and Gratiano's declarations that they are prepared to sacrifice their own lives, together with their wives, to free Antonio. This also prepares us for when the disguised Portia and Nerissa want to obtain the rings they had given their husbands. They want 'revenge' for these words and for the breaking of the ring bond.

**Love versus greed**

### 'The law allows it, and the court awards it'

The moment of triumph for Shylock. All his dreams have come true. He has gained justice according to his bond, and soon his enemy will lie dead. Revenge will be sweet and, presumably, profit even sweeter. But his happiness does not last long, for Portia intervenes just as he is about to cut Antonio's flesh.

**Shylock**

Shylock has placed much store by the letter of the law: the law will give him justice, the law will give him revenge on Antonio, and it will ensure him long-term profit. The very law by which he hoped to gain these aims will prove to be his downfall. We might feel that Portia's interpretation of the law – that it allows flesh to be cut but no blood to flow, – is rather pedantic and perhaps too convenient. However, it ironically picks up her comment to Shylock that he should have provided a surgeon to stop the flow of blood. In this case, it is Portia (the 'surgeon') who effectively stops even a drop of Antonio's blood being split.

> Shylock is triumphant. The law demands the payment of the forfeit. His rejection of Portia's eloquent plea for mercy means that Portia must herself become the 'surgeon' to stop Antonio's blood being spilled. The trial continues.

### Revenge?

Shylock, however, is not only frustrated in his desire to gain revenge. He also suffers at the hands of the law. And one begins to get the uncomfortable feeling that perhaps this time it is Portia and the Christians of Venice who will exact revenge and not temper their justice with mercy.

Shylock may have the forfeiture of his bond and nothing else. If he takes even the merest too much or too little of Antonio's flesh and spills even a drop of Antonio's blood, then he loses his goods and his life. Naturally, he declines and

**Mercy versus justice**

prepares to depart with nothing. However, the law has yet another hold on him.

Because he, a foreigner, conspired to take the life of a Venetian, half his goods must go to Antonio, half to the state of Venice, and his life is at the Duke's mercy.

## Mercy and justice?

**The pound of flesh bond**

Given the extreme penalties that the court could exact from Shylock, perhaps the 'quality of mercy' is demonstrated by the Duke and Antonio. The Duke does not have him executed and Antonio intercedes on his behalf so that the court may 'quit the fine for one half of his goods'. He will use the other and on Shylock's death will give it to Lorenzo, Jessica's husband, to whom will pass every other part of Shylock's wealth.

**Mercy versus justice**

Perhaps the crowning fate is Antonio's demand that Shylock should become a Christian. Again, this is a matter that gives us pause. Is this really mercy? Can it be justified? There is a certain poetic justice to it, given Shylock's well-known opinions and hatred of Christians. Elizabethans may well have seen this as comic retribution to mete out to a non-Christian.

## The ring bond

Anxious to reward the lawyer, Bassanio tries to persuade her to accept the ducats which Shylock had refused. She refuses but, when pressed, wickedly demands the ring she had given him. It is only after he has been persuaded by Antonio that he reluctantly accedes to her demand.

By the end of this long scene, the play's central bond has been resolved and the major themes of 'love and friendship versus greed' and 'mercy versus justice' played out.

**The ring bond**

- Shylock has brought the bond to court and justice has been done
- Antonio's plight has brought his friend Bassanio to his aid but, more importantly, Portia's love for her husband extends to her husband's friends. Love and friendship conspire to frustrate Shylock's greed and hatred
- Shylock refuses to show mercy to Antonio, demanding only 'justice'
- Justice is meted to Shylock by the court and he owes his life to its 'mercy'

# Act 4 Scene 2

*This short, final scene of Act 4 sees Gratiano handing over Bassanio's ring to Portia, and Nerissa retrieving her ring from him.*

The pound of flesh bond has been resolved. Shylock has received justice, but not quite what he had in mind. Antonio is saved: Portia has triumphed. Precious little mercy has been shown, but the letter of the law has been observed. The only matter to be resolved now is the ring bond, but that must take place in Belmont, where love and mercy reign.

# Self-test (Questions) Act Four

## Uncover the plot

Delete two of the three alternatives given, to find the correct plot. Beware possible misconceptions and muddles.

Before the court, Shylock is adamant in his demand for three thousand ducats/ six thousand ducats/the pound of flesh. Bassanio/Balthasar/Bellario tries to encourage Antonio. Portia appears as the lawyer Bellario/Balthasar/ Belmont and after an appeal for justice/the law/mercy, judges that the law is on Antonio's/Shylock's/the Duke's side: the bond must be fulfilled. But there is a catch: since it is not in the bond, Shylock cannot cut the flesh from Antonio's breast/have a surgeon standing by/shed blood. The penalty would be his lands and goods/half his land and goods/his life. Bound by the justice he has demanded, Shylock offers to take 3,000/9,000/36 000 ducats, but – charged with usury/treason/attempted murder of a Venetian – he escapes with his life only through the mercy of the Duke/Antonio/Portia. Portia persuades Bassanio to give her his gloves/purse/ring in thanks. The friends all depart for Padua/Belmont/Venice.

## Who? What? When? Why?

1 Whom does Shylock call a 'noble judge' and 'excellent young man'?
2 What does Shylock refuse to do because it is not in the bond?
3 What is the penalty for an attempt on the life of a Venetian citizen by an alien?
4 What three penalties are finally imposed on Shylock?
5 What do Bassanio and Antonio offer 'Balthasar' for 'his' services – and what does he accept?
6 When has Shylock sworn 'to have the due and forfeit of my bond'?
7 When does 'earthly power show likest God's'?
8 Why is mercy 'twice blest'?
9 Why will 'Balthasar' not 'do a great right, do a little wrong'?
10 Why will 'the deed' to be signed by Shylock be welcome to Lorenzo'?

## Who said that?

1 Who says: 'The pound of flesh which I demand of him/Is dearly bought, 'tis mine and I will have it'?
2 Who says: 'Then must the Jew be merciful' – and what is Shylock's reply?
3 Who says: 'O, be thou damn'd, inexecrable dog!', and to whom?
4 Who says: 'The Jew shall have my flesh, blood, bones and all/Ere thou shalt lose for me one drop of blood', and to whom?
5 Who says: 'He shall have merely justice, and his bond'?

## Open quotes

Find the line – and complete the phrase or sentence.
1 'I do oppose my...to his...and am arm'd/To suffer with a...of.../The very...and...of his.'
2 'For as thou urgest justice, be assur'd...'
3 'The quality of mercy is not strain'd...'
4 'That thou shalt see the difference of our spirit...'

## Prove it!

Find two quotes – one from each of the characters concerned – which could be used to back up the statement that Antonio and Bassanio are willing to die for each other.

## On the other hand

Find a quote from the text that could be used to argue against the following statements.
1 The Duke starts with high hopes that Shylock will be merciful.
2 The Duke starts with no hope that Shylock will be merciful.

## Quick wits

Shylock is a canny opponent. Find the sharp response that follows these appeals.
1 'How shalt thou hope for mercy, rend'ring none?'
2 'Can no prayers pierce thee?'

## Turning-points

Find the lines in the text that mark the crucial turning-points of the trial.
1 In the midst of Shylock's triumph, Portia signals that all is not yet over...
2 Shylock finally relinquishes all claim to the bond, and decides to withdraw...
3 Shylock is utterly defeated...

# Self-test (Answers) Act Four

## Uncover the plot

Before the court, Shylock is adamant in his demand for the pound of flesh. Bassanio tries to encourage Antonio. Portia appears as the lawyer Balthasar and after an appeal for mercy, judges that the law is on Shylock's side: the bond must be fulfilled. But there is a catch: since it is not in the bond, Shylock cannot shed blood. The penalty would be his lands and goods. Bound by the justice he has demanded, Shylock offers to take 9,000 ducats, but – charged with attempted murder of a Venetian – he escapes with his life only through the mercy of the Duke. Portia persuades Bassanio to give her his ring in thanks. The friends all depart for Belmont.

## Who? What? When? Why?

1 Portia/Balthasar 4,1
2 Have a surgeon present to stop Antonio bleeding to death 4,1
3 Half his goods to the intended victim, half to the state, and the offender's life at the Duke's mercy 4,1
4 Half his goods to be held in trust by Antonio for Lorenzo; a deed or 'will' making Lorenzo and Jessica his heirs: conversion to Christianity 4,1
5 3,000 ducats, 'love and service', a 'token': satisfaction, Antonio's gloves and Bassanio's ring 4,1
6 By the Sabbath 4,1
7 When 'justice seasons mercy' 4,1
8 Because it blesses the giver as well as the receiver 4,1
9 Because by comprising Venice's law, dangerous precedents will be set for the future 4,1
10 Because it makes him Shylock's heir 4,2

## Who said that?

1 Shylock 4,1
2 Portia/Balthasar: 'On what compulsion must I?' 4,1
3 Graiano, to Shylock 4,1

## Open quotes

1 'I do oppose my patience to his fury and am arm'd/To suffer with a quietness of spirit/The very tyranny and rage of his.' 4,1
2 'For as thou urgest justice, be assur'd/Thou shalt have justice, more than thou desir'st.' 4,1
3 'The quality of mercy is not strain'd;/It droppeth as a gentle rain from heaven/Upon the place beneath.' 4,1
4 'That thou shalt see the difference of our spirit,/I pardon thee thy life before thou ask it.' 4,1

4 Bassanio, to Antonio 4,1
5 Portia/Balthasar 4,1

## Prove it!

1 Antonio: 'Repent but you that you shall lose your friend,/And he repents not that he pays your debt.' 4,1
2 Bassanio: 'But life itself, my wife and all the world,/Are not with me esteem'd above thy life.' 4,1

## On the other hand

1 'A stony adversary, an inhuman wretch,/Uncapable of pity, void and empty./From any dram of mercy.'
2 ''Tis thought/Thou'lt show thy mercy and remorse, more strange/Than is thy strange apparent cruelty.'

## Quick wits

1 'What judgement shall I dread, doing no wrong?' 4,1
2 'No, none that thou hast wit enough to make.' 4,1

## Turning-points

1 'Tarry a little; there is something else.' 4,1
2 'Why then the devil give him good of it!/I'll stay no longer question.' 4,1
3 'I pray you, give me leave to go from hence;/I am not well...' 4,1

# Act 5 Scene 1

*For the final scene, the action moves to Belmont. Jessica and Lorenzo relax in the moonlight and compare themselves with famous lovers from history and legend. Portia and Nerissa, then Bassanio, Gratiano and Antonio return from Venice. The matter of the rings given to Bassanio and Gratiano is resolved. Antonio offers the final bond and forfeit. A letter gives news that Antonio's ships are safe, and Jessica and Lorenzo hear they are to inherit Shylock's wealth.*

### 'In such a night...'

**The elopement**

We are at Belmont. The trial is over and Antonio is safe. Shylock is defeated, and soon the various parties will return. Lorenzo and Jessica, conjuring up classical images and relaxing in the moonlight, present a scene of peace and happiness only slightly marred by references to 'the wealthy Jew'. But their love for each other and the influence of Belmont is unmistakable, a vivid contrast to the drama of the previous scene.

News is brought that Portia is to return, as will Bassanio. Look at the images presented in Lorenzo's two speeches, 'Sweet soul, let's in...' and 'The reason is, your spirits...'. His praise of music and the harmony it brings encapsulates the spirit of Belmont and its inhabitants.

**Shylock**

Note the words 'The man that hath no music in himself... Is fit for treasons, stratagems...'. This surely refers to Shylock: could such a comment be made of anyone else in the play? Shakespeare has very definite views about man and music. In *Much Ado About Nothing* he likens happy human love to music, 'the true concord of human sound'. In *Julius Caesar*, Caesar observes of Cassius: 'he hears no music... such men... are very dangerous...'.

### 'By yonder moon I swear you do me wrong!'

**The ring bond**

With all the parties returned to Belmont, the ring bond is to be resolved, along with the matters of Antonio's fortune and Shylock's money. Nerissa accuses Gratiano of breaking faith with her, and to make Bassanio squirm a little, Portia declares her husband would never give away a ring she gave him. The ensuing arguments and attempts to justify the giving away of the gifts are never really a serious dispute, but they enable Portia and Nerissa to have some fun at their husbands' expense.

### Another bond

Events, however, come full circle when Antonio intervenes and again offers to enter into a bond for his friend Bassanio, 'I dare be bound again,/My soul upon the forfeit, that your lord/Will never more break faith advisedly.' The forfeit this time, Antonio's soul, is rather more than a pound of flesh. However, in the world of love, friendship and Belmont, there can be no doubt that Antonio will never be called upon to pay the forfeit.

## Tidying up

Portia delivers a letter which reveals that she and Nerissa were the doctor (lawyer) and clerk. She also delivers news that three of Antonio's ships have safely docked and that his fortune is therefore safe. To Jessica and Lorenzo she delivers news of how they shall inherit all of Shylock's wealth when he dies.

The elopement

# Self-test (Questions) Act Five

## Uncover the plot

Delete two of the three alternatives given, to find the correct plot. Beware possible misconceptions and muddles.

In Belmont, Lorenzo and Jessica/Cressida/Nerissa spend the night talking, when Stephano/Solanio/Salerio enters to announce Portia's return, and Launcelot to announce Antonio's/Bassanio's/Gratiano's. In a brief interlude, Lorenzo talks of the 'sweet power' of moonlight/stillness/music. Portia/ Nerissa/Jessica starts a mock argument with Gratiano about his late arrival/ his vehement oaths/his missing ring. Bassanio is drawn in, until Antonio backs him up again – this time with his soul/body/fortune. Portia reveals herself as Bellario/the clerk/the doctor, and with more good news for Lorenzo and Gratiano/Antonio/Shylock, the play ends.

## Who? What? Where? Why?

1 'To whom', 'for whom' and 'for what' did Bassanio give the ring?
2 Who is called 'a kind of boy' – and why is this a joke?
3 What 'becomes' the touches of sweet harmony'?
4 Where does the scene take place?
5 Why is Antonio 'th'unhappy subject of these quarrels'?

## Who said that?

1 Who says: 'Such harmony is in immortal souls'?
2 Who says: 'Sweet lady, you have given me life and living', to whom and why?
3 Who says: 'By heaven, I will ne'er come in your bed/Until I see the ring' – and why is this a joke?

## Open quotes

Find the line – and complete the phrase or sentence.
1 'The man that hath no music in himself...'
2 'I dare be bound again...'
3 'How far that little candle throws his beams!...'

## Odd one out

Pick the odd one out of the following groups – and give a reason for your choice.

1 Portia, Nerissa, Gratiano, Antonio, Jessica, Bassanio, Lorenzo.
2 Music, moonlight, stillness, welcome, harmony, gold.

## General questions on the play

1 What is usury?
2 What are the two main plots, and the two main subplots?
3 List the various 'bonds' given in the play.
4 What is money generally used for a) in Venice and b) in Belmont?
5 In which Act and Scene does Shylock agree the loan?
6 In which Act and Scene does Bassanio choose the lead casket?
7 In which Act and Scene does Jessica elope with Lorenzo?
8 In which Act and Scene does the trial take place?
9 Which two characters mistakenly ask for 'what they deserve' and which two right/ 'give and hazard all they have'?
10 Which three characters most champion mercy, and which of them shows it least in practice?
11 Which two character's turn down an offer of money – and why?
12 When and where is music heard in the play?

## Just for fun

1 Identify: Leah, Margery, Balthasar (the real one!)
2 What is the significance of: Tripolis, the Indies, Mexico and England; Genoa; Frankfort'; the Rialto?
3 What does 'Belmont' mean?
4 List the letters sent in the play.
5 How many times in Act 3 Scene 3 does Shylock say 'I'll have [or 'I will have'] my bond'?

## Uncover the plot

In Belmont, Lorenzo and Jessica spend the night talking, when Stephano enters to announce Portia's return, and Launcelot to announce Bassanio's. In a brief interlude, Lorenzo talks of the 'sweet power' of music. Nerissa starts a mock argument with Graziano about his missing ring. Bassanio is drawn in, until Antonio backs him up again – this time with his soul. Portia reveals herself as the doctor, and with more good news for Lorenzo and Antonio, the play ends.

## Who? What? Where? Why?

1 To the doctor of law, for Antonio, for payment for saving Antonio
2 The clerk – who was really Nerissa, not a boy at all!
3 'Soft stillness and the night'
4 In Portia's garden
5 Because it is on his account that the rings were given to the 'lawyer' and 'clerk'

## Who said that?

1 Lorenzo
2 Antonio, to Portia, because she has given him news that his ships have reached harbour safely
3 Portia – because she is very well aware that she herself is wearing the ring at the time

## Open quotes

1 'The man that hath no music in himself/Is fit for treasons, stratagems, and spoils.'
2 'I dare be bound again./My soul upon the forfeit, that your lord/Will never more break faith advisedly.'
3 'How far that little candle throws his beams!/So shines a good deed in a naughty world.'

## Odd one out

1 Antonio. All the others have paired off at the end
2 Gold. All the others are 'Belmont' words, while gold is associated with Shylock and Venice

## General questions on the play

1 The practice of lending money out at interest

## General questions on the play

1 The practice of lending money out at interest
2 The bond between Antonio and Shylock, and the casket test for Portia's hand. The elopement of Jessica with Lorenzo, and the exchange of rings
3 The pound of flesh bond, the ring bond, and Antonio standing surety for Bassanio's faith with his soul
4 In Venice, for making more money. In Belmont, for hospitality, music and generosity
5 Act 1 Sc 3
6 Act 3 Sc 2
7 Act 2 Sc 6
8 Act 4 Sc 1
9 Prince of Arragon (casket test) and Shylock (trial); Bassanio (casket test) and Antonio (bond)
10 Antonio, the Duke, Portia. Portia is eloquent on the subject of mercy, but shows little to Shylock
11 Shylock – because he refuses to be 'bought off' his bond. Portia (as Balthasar) – because satisfaction is her payment (4, 1)
12 In Belmont, while Bassanio chooses the casket (3, 2). In Belmont, in the final garden scene (5, 1). Plus various trumpet/cornet flourishes for arrivals, both in Venice and Belmont.

## Just for fun

1 Shylock's wife (3, 1), Launcelot's mother (2, 2), Portia's servant (3, 4)
2 Places Antonio's ships are headed! (1, 3); Antonio's Tripolis ship reported wrecked – and Jessica spent fourscore ducats in one night (3, 1); Shylock bought a diamond (3, 1); where all the news is discussed in Venice
3 Beautiful mountain
4 Letter from Antonio to Bassanio (3, 2), letter from Jessica to Lorenzo (2, 3), Letter from Portia to Bellario (3, 4), Letter from Bellario to the Duke (4, 1) – possibly the same as the letter from Bellario used to expose the 'lawyer' plot (5, 1), Letter 'found' by Portia, with news of Antonio's ships (5, 1)
5 Five

# ■ Quotations you should know

The following quotations illustrate aspects of attitude, character and character development, and highlight some of the important themes in the play.

## Antonio

Antonio

While on the one hand demonstrating great love for Bassanio, Antonio also shows a more virulent and abrasive side of his nature when dealing with Shylock. He shows an intelligent recognition of Shylock's nature when, during the negotiation for the loan, he comments on Shylock's tale of Jacob. 'The devil can cite Scripture for his purpose... what a goodly outside falsehood hath!' Some lines later (Act 1 Sc 3, 130), he shows clear understanding of Shylock's likely intentions, 'Who if he break, thou mayst with better face exact the penalty'. He shows blind determination to help his friend, placing faith in the belief that his ships will come home. His attitude to Shylock is sometimes almost naive: 'gentle Jew...'

**'In sooth, I know not why I am so sad'**                          (Act 1 Sc 1, 1)

**'be assur'd my purse, my person, my extremest means
Lie all unlocked to your occasions'**

(to Bassanio, Act 1 Sc 1, 138)

**'Try what my credit can in Venice do:
That shall be rack'd, even to the uttermost'**

(to Bassanio, Act 1 Sc 1, 180)

**'The devil can cite Scripture for his purpose...
O what a goodly outside falsehood hath!'**

(to Bassanio, Act 1 Sc 1, 99–103)

**'I am as like to call thee so (a dog) again,
To spit on thee again, to spurn thee too.
If thou wilt lend this money, lend it not
As to thy friends...
But lend it rather to thine enemy.'**

(to Shylock, Act 1 Sc 1, 130–135)

**'Why fear not man, I will not forfeit it'**     (to Bassanio, Act 1 Sc 1, 157)

'Hie thee, gentle Jew.
The Hebrew will turn Christian: he grows kind.'

(to Bassanio, Act 1 Sc 3, 179–180)

'But stay the very ripening of the time.'

(to Bassanio, Act 2 Sc 8, 40 – Bassanio is told not to hurry back to Venice)

'And even there, his eye being big with tears,...
And with affection wondrous sensible...'
'I think he only loves the world for him'

(Solanio – about Antonio's leave-taking of Bassanio Act 2 Sc 8, 46–50)

'I'll follow him no more with bootless prayers' (Act 3 Sc 3, 26)

'The Duke cannot deny the course of law:' (Act 3 Sc 3, 26)

'...Pray God, Bassanio come
To see me pay his debt, and then I care not.'

(Act 3 Sc 3, 35)

'...I am arm'd and well prepar'd,
Give me your hand, Bassanio: fare you well!
Grieve not that I am fall'n to this for you...
For if the Jew do cut but deep enough,
I'll pay it (the debt) instantly with all my heart.'

(to Bassanio, Act 4 Sc 1, 263–281)

'I once did lend my body for his wealth;
...I dare be bound again,
My soul upon the forfeit, that your lord
Will never more break faith advisedly.'

(to Portia Act 5 Sc 1, 249–253)

## Portia

Portia

Rich, witty, intelligent, and very much in love with Bassanio, Portia demonstrates powerful devotion to the rule of law, and this perhaps explains the merciless determination with which she prosecutes Shylock.

'In Belmont is a lady richly left,
And she is fair and, fairer than that word,
Of wondrous virtues...'

(Bassanio to Antonio Act 1 Sc 1, 161–163)

'I will die as chaste as Diana, unless I be obtained in the manner of my father's will.'

(to Nerissa, Act 1 Sc 2, 116–117)

'But if my father had not scanted me,
And hedg'd me by his wit…'

(to Morocco, Act 2 Sc 1, 17–18)

'To offend, and judge, are distinct offices,
And of opposed natures.'

(to the Prince of Arragon, Act 2 Sc 9, 61–62)

'The quality of mercy is not strain'd,
It droppeth as the gentle rain from heaven
Upon the place beneath: it is twice blest;
It blesseth him that gives, and him that takes:'

(Act 4 Sc 1, 184–187)

'It must not be; there is no power in Venice
Can alter a decree established:
'Twill be recorded for a precedent,
And many an error by the same example
Will rush into the state: it cannot be.'

(Act 4 Sc 1, 218–222)

## Bassanio

Bassanio

Seen as a spendthrift, perhaps, at the beginning of the play,
Bassanio develops and grows in stature as the drama progresses.

'…I have a warranty…
How to get clear of all the debts I owe.'

(to Antonio, Act 1 Sc 1, 132–134)

'I remember him worthy of thy praise.'

(Portia to Nerissa, Act 1 Sc 2, 132)

'You shall not seal to such a bond for me:
I'll rather dwell in my necessity.'

(to Antonio, Act 1 Sc 3, 155–156)

'I like not fair terms, and a villain's mind.'

(to Antonio, Act 1 Sc 3, 181)

'So may the outward shows be least themselves:
The world is still deceived with ornament.
In law, what plea so tainted and corrupt,
But, being seasoned with a gracious voice,
Obscures the show of evil?'

(Act 3 Sc 2, 73–77)

'The Jew shall have my flesh, blood, bones and all,
Ere thou shalt lose for me one drop of blood.'

(to Antonio, Act 4 Sc 1, 112–113)

'To do a great right, do a little wrong,
And curb this cruel devil of his will.'

(to Portia, Act 4 Sc 1, 216–217)

## Shylock and Jessica

Shylock's single-minded greed and cruelty is more than ever apparent when we look closely at his words. Jessica's revulsion at her father's behaviour is also telling.

**'Three thousand ducats; well.'**

(Shylock to Bassanio, Act 1 Sc 3, 1 – the first words that Shylock speaks in the play)

*Shylock*

'I will buy with you, sell with you, talk with you, walk with you, and so following: but I will not eat with you, drink with you, nor pray with you.'

(Shylock to Bassanio, Act 1 Sc 3, 36–39)

'How like a fawning publican he looks!
I hate him for he is a Christian:
But more, for that in low simplicity
He lends out money gratis, and brings down
The rate of usance here with us in Venice.'

(Shylock, Act 2 Sc 3, 42–46)

'You, that did void your rheum upon my beard,
And foot me as you spurn a stranger cur
Over your threshold?'

(Shylock to Antonio, Act 1 Sc 3, 118–120)

'Our house is hell.'      (Jessica to Launcelot, Act 2 Sc 5, 14–15)

'Alack, what heinous sin it is in me
To be ashamed to be my father's child!'

(Jessica, Act 2 Sc 3, 16–17)

'But yet I'll go in hate, to feed upon
The prodigal Christian.'

(Shylock to Jessica , Act 2 Sc 5, 14–15)

'...when you hear the drum
And the vile squealing of the wry-neck'd fife,'

(Shylock to Launcelot, Act 2 Sc 5, 30–31)

'...and if my fortune be not crost,
I have a father, you a daughter, lost'

(Jessica, Act 2 Sc 5, 56–57)

'wise, fair, and true.'

(Lorenzo on Jessica, Act 2 Sc 6, 56)

' "My daughter! O my ducats! O my daughter!
Fled with a Christian! O my Christian ducats!
Justice! the law! my ducats, and my daughter!" '

(Solanio, quoting Shylock, Act 2 Sc 8, 15–18)

'...and what's his reason (for his treatment of me)? I am a Jew.
Hath not a Jew eyes? ... and if you wrong us shall we not take revenge?'

(Shylock to Salerio, Act 3 Sc 1, 52–64 NB You should know
the main points of this speech)

'I would my daughter were dead at my foot, and the jewels in her ear!
would she were hears'd at my foot, and the ducats in her coffin!'

(Shylock to Tubal, Act 3 Sc 1, 89–91)

'I will have the heart of him if he forfeit, for were he out of Venice I can
make what merchandise I will.'

(Shylock to Tubal, Act 3 Sc 1, 132–134)

'...tell me not of mercy'

(Shylock to the Gaoler, Act 3 Sc 1, 132–134)

'How shalt thou hope for mercy, rend'ring none?'

(The Duke to Shylock, Act 4 Sc 1, 88)

'The man that hath no music in himself,
Nor is not moved with concord of sweet sounds,
Is fit for treasons, stratagems, and spoils;
...
Let no such man be trusted.'

(Lorenzo, Act 5 Sc 1, 83–88)

## Gratiano

Despite his rude and wild nature, Gratiano displays some clear perception about
the world he lives in, and the dangers to Antonio.

'There are a sort of men whose visages
Do cream and mantle like a standing pond,
And do a wilful stillness entertain.'

(Gratiano to Antonio, Act 1 Sc 1, 88–90)

'Gratiano speaks an infinite deal of nothing, more than any man in Venice. His reasons are as two grains of wheat hid in two bushells of chaff.'

(Bassanio to Antonio, Act 1 Sc 1, 190–196)

'Thou art too wild, too rude, and bold of voice;
...allay with some cold drops of modesty
Thy skipping spirit,'

(Bassanio to Gratiano, Act 2 Sc 2, 190–196)

## The casket bond

The casket test

' "Who chooseth me, shall gain what many men desire." '

(inscription on the gold casket)

' "Who chooseth me, shall gain as much as he deserves." '

(inscription on the silver casket)

' "Who chooseth me must give and hazard all he hath." '

(inscription on the lead casket)
(Act 2 Sc 7)

Note that on the gold and silver caskets, the emphasis is on 'gain', but on the lead casket it is on 'give'. The former are to do with greed, the latter with love.

'All that glisters is not gold;
Often have you heard that told:
Many a man his life hath sold
But my outside to behold:
Gilded tombs do worms infold,'

(the scroll within the gold casket, Act 2 Sc 7, 65–69)

'First, never to unfold to anyone
Which casket 'twas I chose; next, if I fail
of the right casket never in my life
To woo a maid in way of marriage:
Lastly,
If I do fail in fortune of my choice,
Immediately to leave you, and be gone.

(Prince of Arragon, Act 2 Sc 9, 10–16)

# Writing an examination essay

## Take the following to heart

- *Carefully study each of the questions set on a particular text* Make sure you understand what they are asking for so that you select the one you know most about.
- *Answer the question* Obvious, isn't it? But bitter experience shows that many students fail because they do not actually answer the question that has been set.
- *Answer all the question* Again, obvious, but so many students spend all their time answering just part of a question and ignoring the rest. This prevents you gaining marks for the parts left out.

## The question

1 Read and understand every word of it. If it asks you to compare (the similarities) and/or contrast (the differences) between characters or events, then that is what you must do.
2 Underline all the key words and phrases that mention characters, events and themes, and all instructions as to what to do, e.g. compare, contrast, outline, comment, give an account, write about, show how/what/where.
3 Now write a short list of the things you have to do, one item under the other. A typical question will only have between two and five items at most for you to cope with.

## Planning your answer

1 Look at each of the points you have identified from the question. Think about what you are going to say about each. Much of it will be pretty obvious, but if you think of any good ideas, jot them down before you forget them.
2 Decide in what order you are going to deal with the question's major points. Number them in sequence.
3 So far you have done some concentrated, thoughtful reading and written down maybe fifteen to twenty words. You know roughly what you are going to say in response to the question and in what order – if you do not, you have time to give serious thought to trying one of the other questions.

## Putting pen to paper

The first sentences are important. Try to summarise your response to the question so the examiner has some idea of how you are going to approach it. Do not say 'I am going to write about the character of Macbeth and show how evil he was' but instead write 'Macbeth was a weak-willed, vicious traitor. Totally dominated by his "fiend-like queen" he deserved the epitaph "this dead butcher" or did he?' Jump straight into the essay, do not nibble at its extremities for a page and a half. High marks will be gained by the candidate who can show he or she has a mind engaged with the text. Your personal response is rewarded – provided you are answering the question!

As you write your essay *constantly refer back to your list of points* and make sure you are actually responding to them.

## How long should it be?

There is no 'correct' length. What you must do is answer the question set, fully and sensitively in the time allowed. Allocate time to each question according to the percentage of marks awarded of it.

## How much quotation or paraphrase?

Use only that which is relevant and contributes to the quality and clarity of your answer. Padding is a waste of your time and gains not a single mark.